The International Dimension in the National Curriculum

Rex Andrews

**Trentham Books/
Marc Goldstein Memorial Trust**

First published in 1994 by Trentham Books Limited

Trentham Books Limited
Westview House
734 London Road
Oakhill
Stoke-on-Trent
Staffordshire
England ST4 5NP

British Library Cataloguing Publication Data
A catalogue record for this book is available from the British Library.

ISBN: 0 948080 62 0

Designed and typeset by Trentham Print Design Limited
and printed by Bemrose Shafron Limited, Chester.

The International Dimension in the
National Curriculum

Mathew Arnold (1822-1888) HM Inspector of Schools
(1951-1986)

'Criticism... a disinterested endeavour to learn and propagate the best that is known and thought in the world, and thus to establish a current of fresh and true ideas. By the very nature of things, as England is not all the world, much of the best that is known and thought in the world cannot be of English growth, must be foreign; by the nature of things, again, it is just this that we are least likely to know... The English critic, therefore, must dwell much on foreign thought...'

Bronze sculpture by Kate Andrews (1958-1985)

Contents

Acknowledgements   ix

The Author   xi

Foreword by Professor Denis Lawton   xiii

Chapter 1:   1
The Setting
Introduction to the purpose, scope and limitations of the
study. Qualified welcome to the National Curriculum.
Education for global citizenship

Chapter 2:   11
History, Glasnost and Perestroika
A changing world; educational implications. History
programme of the National Curriculum

Chapter 3:   27
The Core Subjects (1) English Language
Language in the National Curriculum. Communication;
individual language mastery; discrimination; writing

Chapter 4:   43
The Core Subjects (2) Maths and Science
Pure maths — a universal language. Its international
origins. Applied maths — universal implications.
B. Science: a universal quest. Breadth, balance and
international relevance

Chapter 5:   61
The Foundation Subjects (1)
Geography, Technology, a Modern Foreign Language.
(nb for History v. Chap. 2)

Chapter 6:   85
The Foundation Subjects (2)
Art, Music, Physical Education (including Sport and
Olympic Games)

Chapter 7:   109
Religious Education and Citizenship in a Plural Society
Issues for education and community relations. Alternative
of secularism to reconcile differences. Pluralism and the
integration of identities. Human Rights and RE. Religion
and education in France, USA, Poland, etc

Chapter 8:   127
Literature for a New World Order
Principles. Value of imaginative literature and wide
reading. What is 'national culture'? Close reading.
Principles of choice.

Chapter 9:   143
Literature for a New World Order
A range of material world-wide literature for each of the
Key Stages.

Chapter 10:   161
Conclusion: What of the Future?
The responsibility of teachers to deliver a 'humanised'
curriculum. The National Curriculum neither a gag nor a
strait-jacket for the globally-minded teacher, but a
challenge.

Appendix 1: Universal Declaration of Human Rights   167

Appendix 2: Seville Statement on Violence   173

Bibliography, Recommended reading, listed by chapters.   177

Index   183

Acknowledgements

A book of this kind cannot be written without the help and encouragement of many colleagues, and is heavily dependent on the groundwork laid by numerous workers in the same field. It would never have been written but for my friendship with and profound respect for a former colleague, Marc Goldstein, to whose memory it is dedicated.

For recent help throughout I must, in particular, thank Dr Jagdish Gundara, Head of the Centre of Multicultural Education in the University of London Institute of Education, to whom I am indebted also for specific contributions to Chapters 7 and 9, which embody so many incorporations of his actual words along with mine that they should be regarded as being jointly written. Also the section on Art in Chapter 6, and the 'Principles of Choice', at the end of Chapter 8 are based heavily on help from Dr Gundara.

For advice on the first draft of the chapter on History I am much indebted to Dr John Slater, formerly HMI with special responsibilities in that area. To Dr David Hicks, whose work on education for international understanding and futures studies is well known, I owe special thanks for material he has provided which has been useful throughout.

Colleagues in the University of London Institute of Education where I have been fortunate enough to have a Visiting Fellowship for the past five years have been very helpful. In particular I wish to acknowledge the support of the former Director, Professor Denis Lawton, and the current Director, Sir Peter Newsam; and of fellow Trustees of the Marc Goldstein Memorial Trust, Professor Norman Graves and the late Dr Anthony Weaver.

For scrupulous care with the editing of my draft, and for further ideas and encouragement I must thank Gillian Klein of Trentham Books. To John Stipling I owe thanks for dealing with the complexities of layout.

I am conscious that there are many others to whom I am indebted, not least to students and pupils I have taught as well as to colleagues, and ask their indulgence if I have omitted to mention them by name. I must, however, take full responsibility for the publication as it stands, and any errors or shortcomings are mine and not my colleagues'.

Finally, publication of this book would not have been possible without a generous grant from the Joseph Rowntree Charitable Trust for which the Trustees of the Marc Goldstein Trust would like to express their joint appreciation.

The Author

Rex Andrews, BA(Hons), MPhil, PhD, was Principal Lecturer in English at the University of London Goldsmiths' College and subsequently Visiting Fellow at the University of London Institute of Education.

He taught in UK state primary and secondary schools for some ten years and in colleges of education and university for twenty years. Since taking early retirement he lives in France where he teaches English as a Foreign Language and writes.

Editor of the *London Educational Review* from 1971-1974 and a member of the University of London Institute of Education Publications Sub-Committee for ten years, he is author of numerous articles on English teaching, the media, the arts, and education for international understanding.

As a member of the World Education Fellowship (of which he was Chairman of the Great Britain section from 1983-1986) and the World Council for Curriculum and Instruction he has contributed to numerous conferences world-wide, and has had the good fortune to see schools in action in Australia, Canada, Czechoslovakia, France, India, Indonesia, Japan, the Netherlands, Nigeria, the Philippines, Sweden, Thailand and the USA.

Following a specialist lecture tour for the British Council in India, he is a life member of AWIC (the Association of Writers and Illustrators for Children), New Delhi.

He was Honorary Secretary of the Marc Goldstein Memorial Trust to promote education for international understanding from its foundation until the present time, and is currently the World Education Fellowship NGO Representative at Unesco, Paris, and a Fellow of the Royal Society of Arts, London.

Foreword

Since the Education Reform Act was passed in 1988 discussions about education in England have been dominated by arguments about the national curriculum. In this book, Dr Rex Andrews makes a very significant contribution to that debate.

He begins by voting for only two cheers for the national curriculum. I would heartily agree: some kind of national consensus on curriculum entitlement 5-16 was long overdue. But the 1988 national curriculum entitlement was disappointing in many respects. Rex Andrews wisely resists the temptation to dwell on the shortcomings of the national curriculum but, instead, writes constructively about what can be done by schools and teachers to make sure that an international dimension can emerge.

Rex Andrews accomplishes that quite brilliantly, showing a real understanding of the complexities of curriculum design, as well as detailed knowledge of the subjects in the current national curriculum. It is a most worthwhile piece of work, and I am sure that teachers will be grateful to him, whatever their own subject might be.

Denis Lawton
December 1993
London

Chapter 1

The Setting

Education shall be directed to the full development of the human person-ality and to the strengthening of respect for human rights and fun-damental freedoms. It shall promote understanding, tolerance and friendship among nations, racial or religious groups and shall further the activities of the United Nations for the maintenance of peace. (Universal Declaration of Human Rights, Article 26(2))

Oh, East is East, and West is West, and never the twain shall meet. (Rudyard Kipling)

I am not conscious of a single experience throughout my three months stay in England and Europe that made me feel that after all East is East and West is West. On the contrary, I have been convinced more than ever that human nature is much the same, no matter under what clime it flourishes.... (Mahatma Gandhi)

The Peace Bell, Hiroshima, on the site of the Peace Memorial Park constructed in the area devasted by the A-bomb on August 6th 1945. A world map with no national boundaries symbolising 'One World' is engraved on the surface of the bell.

'No man is an island, entire of itself; every man is a piece of the continent, a part of the main; if a clod be washed away by the sea, Europe is the less, as well as if a promontory were, as well as if a manor of thy friends or of thine own were; any man's death diminishes me, becasue I am involved in mankind. And therefore never send to know for whom the bell tolls. It tolls for thee' John Donne: Devotions upon Emergent Occasions, 1624

1. Purpose, scope and limitations of the present study

This book is addressed to teachers, prospective teachers, heads, governors, inspectors and all others who recognise that schools have a responsibility to provide a dimension of international understanding and a concern for conflict resolution in their programmes, and who want reassurance that the National Curriculum provides opportunities for this. Perhaps contrary to expectations, many of the ideals of peace educators are actually embedded in areas of the new curriculum, and there are of course spaces left for independent initiatives by teachers and headteachers. Creative teachers, in any case, recognise that process is equally as important as content, and that vital attitudes depend as much on the way subject-matter is taught as upon the syllabus content itself.

The United Kingdom in common with other members of the United Nations is formally committed to the principles of the Universal Declaration of Human Rights, including Article 26(2) on education quoted above. Recent events in Eastern Europe, in the Gulf, in Yugoslavia and in Somalia have heightened the significance and relevance of these aims. Global awareness and the reality of interdependence are gradually dawning on us. An oil slick in the Arabian Gulf, a nuclear reactor failure in Russia, a peaceful revolution in Eastern Europe, or a violent one, a recession in America, a war in Africa, a famine in the Far East: these affect all of us either directly or indirectly. Tourism and air travel are inhibited by wars and by terrorism. The transmission of information, weaponry, supplies and disease has accelerated world-wide. Clearly today, 'no man is an island'.

Not surprisingly, attitudes to war are steadily changing. The so-called 'Great War' saw thousands of young men eager to give up their lives for a patriotic ideal: 'Dulce et decorum est pro patria mori' (It is sweet and fitting to die for one's native land), while a flurry of white feathers was directed at those unwilling to join in the butchery. In World War II men and women readily sacrificed their lives to bring down an evil dictatorship that was spreading like a cancer throughout Europe and beyond. But the Gulf War revealed signs of a new perspective. We have seen soldiers interviewed on television ready to fight 'if necessary', but admitting their fears, and their hopes of a negotiated settlement. The aggression and atrocities of the 'enemy' are recognised, but seen in a wider context of the despotism and corruption acknowledged to be endemic in the world — and in which we are all to some extent implicated. So by what values are we now to choose and change our allies as circumstances alter? And can humankind any longer afford to have enemies beyond the destructive demons buried in our own psyche? Whose messages do we believe in a war, when the first value to be set aside is inevitably Truth, as freedom of information gives way to secrecy, censorship and 'disinformation'? And when the second value abolished is respect for human life and dignity as we watch on television the tragic consequences of 'collateral damage' to innocent civilians? Educators need to be able to help young people find their way through these questionings. While not losing sight of the best ideals that have been transmitted from the past, they must take account of new attitudes, new insights and new possibilities.

In examining the National Curriculum for the elements within it that can help to promote concern for Human Rights and international understanding the author is well aware of having taken on a somewhat formidable task; and so it is important here to give the reasons for attempting such an overview, together with an indication of the limitations that must be recognised in an enterprise of this kind. There are, and will continue to be, many books about the different separate subjects of the curriculum; and there are various books available geared specifically to the primary or secondary level. Similarly, there is a range of books on international understanding, conflict resolution and human rights written in pre-National Curriculum days. But since the new curriculum, in the early days at least, might very well engulf the whole school timetable, it seemed highly necessary to examine the situation of the international dimension from within the new context either to reassure those who recognise the importance of this element or to raise the alarm before the new mixture sets too hard.

Obviously, it is not possible to cover every relevant aspect of every subject at every level in a book of this size; but an attempt has been made to test the temperature, so to speak, at various key points throughout the range, and assess the general orientation and potential within the new framework. The task has been complicated by the mobility and unpredictability of the subject-matter hitherto, and several chapters have had to be re- written to cope with ministerial changes between the Working Groups' 'Final' reports and the statutory versions. But now the baby has been born and we must try to ensure its healthy development! Hence this post-natal examination and critique.

2.   Two cheers for the National Curriculum

On the whole, the National Curriculum is not the monster that might have been feared. The period of its gestation was exactly sixteen years, and it is essentially the product of both major political parties. Although it has finally emerged under the Conservatives, it was a Labour Prime Minister who started off the whole process:

> Since Sir James Callaghan's speech as Prime Minister at Ruskin College in 1976, successive Secretaries of State have aimed to achieve agreement with their partners in the education service on policies for the school curriculum which will develop the potential of all pupils and equip them for the responsibilities of citizenship and for the challenges of employment in tomorrow's world. (DES, 1987)

There is no point in speculating about what the curriculum would have been like under a different political regime. The fact remains that something needed to be done to tidy up the educational system. In keeping with the spirit of the times, the new regulations exemplify the 'openness' of *glasnost* in that the curriculum has now emerged from 'the secret garden' of arbitrary school arrangements into the light of public scrutiny. (Although the openness in this case is coupled with a reduction rather than an enlargement of individual freedom.) The rather anarchic curricular practice of British schools in the past has for some time needed the corrective of something in the way of national guide-lines. Some schools, it must be admitted, provided too little in the way of a working framework to guide new entrants to the teaching profession. And there was always the problem of continuity from school to school. Another major problem, recognised for some time by critics such as C.P. Snow (1964) and W.D. Wall (1977), was that premature specialisation producing either 'arts' or 'science' students was warping the English education system. H.J.A. Hargreaves (1970) pointed out that the tendency towards early specialisation was not only immoral but also inappropriate, for:

> the person who finds that his specialised knowledge is obsolescent, and has no particular facility to learn, has the ground cut from beneath his feet. Although this is a scientific age... science must be tempered and balanced by an understanding of the humanities.... As in other crucial periods of history, there is a need for whole men and not split personalities.

Accordingly, the Education Reform Act wisely seeks to entitle:

> ...every pupil in maintained schools... to a curriculum which is balanced and broadly based and which... (a) promotes the spiritual, moral, cultural, mental and physical development of pupils at the school and of society; and (b) prepares such pupils for the opportunities, responsibilities and experiences of adult life. (DES, 1989)

The balance is to be achieved by the three core subjects: English, mathematics and science; seven other foundations subjects: history, geography, technology, music, art, physical education and a modern foreign language; plus 'non-denominational religious education'. However, it is recognised that 'the foundation subjects are certainly not a complete curriculum' and among other elements stated to be needed are: 'coverage across the curriculum of gender and multicultural issues' and 'a range of themes which might be taught in a cross-curricular way such as economic awareness, political and international understanding, and environmental education...' (D.E.S. 1989). A further section affirms that:

> There will be a great deal of scope for teachers in schools to carry out curriculum development without cutting across the statutory requirements — indeed, the introduction of the National Curriculum seems likely to stimulate a lot of work at local level on aspects of the contents of the curriculum and its organisation and to help focus this on the essentials of what teachers and pupils need. (ibid.)

All this seems very much to the point. Why, then, only two cheers for the new curriculum?

2. Some problems of the new arrangements

The main problem is perhaps the unequal delivery of the package: there is nothing for some and too much for the others. The private education sector does not come under the new regulations and so can carry on doing just as it likes. (Is this punishment by deprivation, or favouritism?) The public sector, on the other hand, gets so much of it — about 80% of timetabled time — that the 'range of themes' and other 'cross-curricular' material mentioned above might well be squeezed out. The weight of the testing arrangements, at 7, 11, 14 and 16 years is a further constraint upon teaching time, with the added snag that schools or teachers feeling vulnerable because of the competition and the public way in which the results are intended to be used, may well put in extra time on the Foundation Subjects, thus reducing even further their capacity for individual creativity and initiative. 'The National Curriculum Attainment Targets have been designed so that a typical pupil will move up one level approximately every two years' (DES 1991). The 'typical' pupil is of course the (abstract) 'average' pupil; and since half the population is necessarily below average there will be a lot of people (parents, if not children) worried about grades.

> We are suffering from an excessive development of the competitive system.... Education, instead of consisting in a careful and systematic development of the faculties, is in danger of reducing itself to preparing children for a series of spasmodic efforts... (and)... the whole theory of education becomes disturbed.

This was in a letter to the Editor of the *Pall Mall Gazette* on October 5, 1870. Matthew Arnold, perhaps the most illustrious of Her Majesty's Inspectors of Schools, was worried about the 'mental gymnastics' and 'the art of catching marks' involved in the notorious 'Payment by Results' system then in vogue. Elsewhere he wrote that as a result of the system, 'the children's reading has thus been narrowed and impoverished all the year for the sake of a *result* at the end of it, and the result is an illusion.' With our new system of '*Judgement* by Results', the object of national tests 'demanding national targets for pupils of all ages and abilities' is 'to achieve higher standards'. It is not at all clear how this improvement is to take place: tests will simply show (or rather attempt to show) what the standards are; they cannot raise them.

I am not objecting here to the setting of standards; it is helpful for teachers to have guidelines as to what might be expected of their pupils at given periods in their education. There has hitherto been a lack of helpful touchstones of this kind. What I find unreasonable is forcing everyone to jump through the hoops like trained circus animals, and then, whatever the catchment area or circumstances prevailing in the different schools, to publish the results as though they represented some genuine comparisons. Someone once said, (oddly enough in *Much Ado About Nothing*) that 'Comparisons are odorous'(sic!). Certainly, these comparisons will be fishy!

However, whatever the problems of the National Curriculum, teachers are obliged to work with it. Its heavy-handed introduction did not make its reception as easy as it might have been; and the anxiety attaching to the need to comply with so many restrictions of subject-matter and testing will undoubtedly restrict initiative and creative spontaneity for a while. But there is no reason to suppose that this will last for ever, nor is there need for excessive inhibition even now. Once the parameters are mastered it is likely that a degree of freedom and creativity will be achieved within them; that space will be found for innovation in the gaps; and that modifications of subject-matter and testing procedures will be achieved as the curriculum becomes humanised. Teachers cannot operate successfully as automatons, and the system to be successful must adapt eventually to what is humanly possible and practicable. By mid-1993, for example prompted by Sir Ron Dearing's Inquiry, the government had modified the requirements considerably, so that schools now have 20-33% of time to allocate to non-statutory curriculum areas. It is reasonable to anticipate further modifications in the future.

4. Education for global citizenship

At least in its margins, the National Curriculum acknowledges the importance of good citizenship, and the National Curriculum Council in its pamphlet *Education for Citizenship* (1990) offers some suggestions. These include teaching about 'the nature of community' so that: 'Pupils should develop knowledge and understanding of... the variety of communities to which people simultaneously belong: family, school, local, national, European and worldwide'. This is a welcome acknowledgement of global interdependence. The document also includes reference to the importance of reconciliation, co-operation, 'diversity and independence' and 'the rule of custom and law in prescribing duties, responsibilities and rights'. Among the 'positive attitudes' to be promoted in schools 'if pupils are to value democracy and its associated duties, responsibilities and rights' are: 'independence of thought on social and moral issues'; ' respect for different

Part of the Headquarters of UNESCO, Paris

ways of life, beliefs, opinions and ideas'; 'respect for rational argument and non-violent ways of resolving conflict'; and 'an active concern for human rights'. It is good to have official confirmation that these issues are regarded as important, even if the time available for them may be limited.

This aspect of the National Curriculum, and the teachers who implement it, have the support of a number of official documents. The first of these is the Department of Education and Science Circular Number 9/76 from which the following extract comes:

At its Eighteenth Session in 1974, the General Conference of UNESCO adopted the recommendation concerning education for international understanding, co-operation and peace and education relating to human rights and fundamental freedoms...

The Secretaries of State attach importance to the message of the recommendation having the widest possible dissemination and impact and look to all those to whom this circular is addressed to consider the best ways in which, in their local circumstances, the recommendation can be used.

The Secretaries of State expressed themselves to be confident that the response would be 'both sympathetic and constructive'; but as to the matter of resources, — manpower, equipment and money — they hoped that 'the recommendation can be achieved by the adaptation of existing resources without creating demands for new ones'. This Circular was sent to all Local Education Authorities and Voluntary Colleges of Education, and to my knowledge has never been rescinded. More recently, on 14 May 1985, the Council of Europe Committee of Ministers issued Recommendation No. R(85)7 on 'Teaching and Learning about Human Rights in Schools', a four-page document which includes (among other things) under the heading 'Human rights in the school curriculum':

> The understanding and experience of human rights is an important element of the preparation of all young people for life in a democratic and pluralistic society. It is part of social and political education, and it involves intercultural and international understanding.

Detailed suggestions for the implementation of this follow in the document. There is also the *European Convention on Human Rights*, and of course the *Universal Declaration of Human Rights* itself (see Appendix 1), to which the United Kingdom is a signatory.

In 1989 the Children Act and the subsequent relevant Guidance and Regulations, Volume 2 provided further legal backing for those concerned to promote tolerance and eliminate racial discrimination. The Guidance issued by the Department of Health refers to the importance of knowledge of and attitudes to multicultural issues and people of different racial origins; (and) commitment and knowledge to treat all children as individuals and with equal concern'.

The Children Act — for a further discussion of which see Lane (1992) — rightly recognises that children begin to pick up racial attitudes and values at a very early age.

At the Commonwealth Heads of Government Meeting in Harare (October 1991) a long *Communique* was issued spelling out the Commonwealth's future role in the contemporary world. It included the passage:

> (Heads of Government)...were convinced that, in facing the challenges of the future, the Commonwealth would draw upon its unique strength and character, rooted in its shared ideals, common traditions and language, in its membership which spans nearly one-third of humanity and every corner of the globe and in its ability to fashion a sense of common purpose out of diversity.

All too often the links and facilities of Commonwealth membership are overlooked in considerations of intercultural and international understanding, but the Commonwealth Secretariat and, in particular, the Commonwealth Institute in London, can be a great resource to teachers working in this area.

Finally it should be remembered, even while Britain remains outside official membership, that the substantial resources of UNESCO, founded in 1946 with Professor Julian Huxley as its first Director-General are always available to teachers concerned to improve their global perspective.

Chapter 2

History, Glasnost and Perestroika

Today the whole world needs restructuring, to experience progressive development, a fundamental change.
(Mikhael Gorbachev: Perestroika)

History has much to offer education for the future. Firstly, it is the only subject in the curriculum to have time as its prime concern and, secondly, the future is very much rooted in the past. Yesterday's local, national and world history not only gives us the present but also has a major influence on the approaching future.
(David Hicks: Exploring Alternative Futures)

Freedom is the right to tell people what they do not want to hear.
(George Orwell: The Road to Wigan Pier)

1. A changing world

When the plan for the National Curriculum was first conceived nobody in Britain had heard of *glasnost* or *perestroika*. But in half a decade their influence has engendered a movement that has banished the Cold War, changed the face of Europe and fundamentally altered global politics. Incidentally (though not surprisingly) the terms found their way right into the original version of the History programme of the National Curriculum itself, until the then Secretary of State for Education declared that history stopped twenty years ago. Although they have had to be removed as anachronisms within the official time-scale, their significance remains. What precisely do these two preg-nant terms signify? What is their bearing on education in general and on the National Curriculum in particular? And what implications do the terms now have as regards global citizenship?

Glasnost, sometimes freely translated as 'transparency' or 'openness', is based on a Russian root related to speech — hence its essential meaning: 'free speech'. In response to Mikhail Gorbachev's initiative in promoting the concept, '*Glasnost*' was the name given to the in-dependent journal which first appeared in Russia in July 1987 under the editorship of S. Grigoriants, significantly a dissident then newly released from imprisonment. Its object was to make redundant the need for the underground circulation of '*samizdat*' by creating a forum for open social criticism. The aim of *glasnost* was to lift taboos, reduce the element of secretiveness in government and create genuine dialogue. Open critical evaluation of social and political practices, it was hoped, would create a climate of accountability and lead in turn to action to reduce waste and abuse of power. It has certainly led to a great deal of change.

'*Perestroika*' was meant to be the active counterpart of *glasnost* — the 'restructuring' of society and political relations as a result of critical re-examination. It implied new thinking, the adoption of new per-spectives and a revolutionary transformation of society. In his book *Perestroika: new thinking for our country and the world* (1987), Mikhail Gorbachev stressed the two critical priorities to which *perestroika* was addressed: the furtherance of international peace and co-operation, and a decisive acceleration in social and economic development in the USSR and the world at large. It sought improvement in production, mutual international support, the reversal of the Arms Race, tolerance of diversity, amelioration of human rights abuses, and co-operative concern for the global environment. It was not regarded as an easy panacea: Gorbachev recognised from the start that its application

By Dana Summers 1990, Washington Post Writers Group

would be both 'novel and difficult'. But it was necessary. 'We are entering an era in which progress will be based on the common interests of the whole of humankind,' he declared in the key address he gave at the United Nations on December 7th 1988, and 'the realisation of this fact demands that the common values of humanity must be the determining priority in international politics.' The address concluded: 'I hope our joint efforts to end the epoch of wars, confrontation and regional conflicts, to end aggression against Nature, the terror of hunger and poverty and political terrorism will justify our aspirations' (Gorbachev, 1988).

Certainly the path opened up by *glasnost* and *perestroika* was far from smooth. On the credit side, mass non-violent demonstrations brought about the dismantling of the Berlin Wall and allowed the reunification of Germany; similar peaceful demonstrations of people-power in former Czechoslovakia, and in Poland and Hungary have brought substantial moves towards democracy; the neo-Stalinist regime in Romania has been weakened; the arms race between the Superpowers has been reversed; and the ex-USSR has begun an era of co-operation

13

with Western Europe and America. On the debit side hopes for economic improvement in Russia and the other former Soviet states have not materialised fast enough for the population, and Gorbachev's adoption of an increasingly authoritarian stance against the growing opposition of his own people led to the resignation of his Foreign Minister, Eduard Shevardnadze, and to Gorbachev's displacement by the Russian Prime Minister, Boris Yeltsin, whose own position has been far from secure. The independence of the Baltic states; disturbances in Armenia; and even the tragic events of Tienenman Square in China, and the eruption of violence in Yugoslavia — all these things, among many others, have embarrassed Gorbachev's position and clouded his remarkable achievements. Uncertainties about unrestricted market forces, increasing unemployment and reduced social security must be weighed against such benefits as more free speech, open communication and increasing freedom to travel in former Warsaw Pact countries.

There can be little doubt that *glasnost* and *perestroika* were necessary purgatives for ills both internally within the former Soviet Union and internationally. *Perestroike* as originally envisioned by Gorbachev is over, though its reverberations are not; and *glasnost*, at least, will continue to bring positive global benefits, since 'openness', despite the problems and challenges it implies, is a necessary element of democracy. Educators world-wide cannot ignore these changes. The bolder profile and increased importance of the United Nations is by no means the least of the many significant developments resulting from Gorbachev's initiatives. Whether the United Nations can successfully fulfil the heavy demands of its important new role will depend largely upon the support it receives from the international community; and this in turn depends upon the appropriate education of the oncoming generation of young people.

2. Educational implications

It is an interesting paradox resulting from *glasnost* and *perestroika* that as teachers' freedom has been curtailed in the United Kingdom, the reverse is happening in the ex-Soviet Union. Teachers there have more freedom to work as they wish; they are experimenting with different methods; and even sometimes consulting their pupils about course content (Poppleton, 1990). Apparently, in the USSR 'Most teachers (72% according to a recent survey) desire changes in the school and are in favour of educational reconstructing, but half of them do not know what needs to be done and how' (ibid. p.95). Also, for many teachers the shortage of textbooks and teaching aids makes the development of individualised courses difficult and frustrating. One teacher spoke of improved opportunities and greater choice even within the then existing, unchanged curriculum:

> If... we are discussing different authors in the literature we can interpret them in a more democratic way. Also relations have improved. (The pupils) have become more open, more frank and they trust me and I somehow rely on them and it makes me feel satisfied. (ibid.p.96)

This teacher 'loves her work' and would not change jobs for more money; but some teachers are taking advantage of the incipient market economy, changing to part-time evening teaching in commercial cooperatives for increased salary and thus creating staffing problems as they leave their regular day-teaching posts.

Particularly interesting developments are occurring in history teaching:

> In the new atmosphere of openness it is not surprising that the re-interpretation of history becomes a pressing problem. Nationalist feeling gives this a particular edge in Latvia and Georgia, but all Soviet schools are faced with the problem of re-constructing history now that the official version has been abandoned. (ibid.p.94)

A new two-volume history textbook *Our Native Land* has now appeared challenging the teachings of generations of communist ideology. The Tsarist rule, the Revolution, the Stalinist purges, the idols of the Soviet system, and even the coming and going of *perestroika* itself, have been re-examined with a new critical objectivity. 'The time has passed', say the publishers, 'when we had one leader, one party, one ideology and one textbook.'

This observation adds to the significance of the warning by our own National Curriculum History Working Group in their *Final Report* (April 1990) that we ourselves must beware of the danger of creating an 'official' version of *our* history! But to return to the USSR, the Director of Schools in the Riga district observed that when teachers were given additional freedom to teach 'as they saw fit' in certain secondary schools with severe discipline problems, 'Good teachers teach better under *perestroika* but poor teachers do worse'(p.96) 'This raises a perennial question in relation to formal 'authoritarian' versus informal 'progressive' methods. Many an inadequately prepared teacher or student attempting child-centred project or similar work in the belief that it was somehow easier or required less organisation, has found the resulting anarchy and disruptive behaviour too much to cope with and has resorted to authoritarian severity in sheer self-defence. This pattern is perhaps a microcosmic reflection of Mikhail Gorbachev's larger experience: *glasnost* — anarchy — authoritarian retrenchment. This is not an argument against open and progressive methods; but an argument for careful preparation and a full under-standing of the complexities of informal teaching organisation. *Glasnost* with its accompanying freedoms is, in the classroom as well as the state, both an 'open Sesame' and 'Pandora's Box'. It needs careful handling.

3. National Curriculum History programme: original version

As far as the History programme of the National Curriculum is con-cerned, the History Working Group's original *Final Report* (1990), by careful handling, managed to make quite a respectable 'silk purse' out of a 'pig's ear' of a brief. The greatest challenge was to avoid the mandatory Attainment Targets dominating the whole enterprise; and the group almost succeeded in this. I say 'almost' because the need to establish a matrix of ten levels for four basic targets resulted in some astonishingly subtle, not to say arbitrary, distinctions. The application of 'Occam's razor' ('Entities are not to be multiplied without necessity') would have been welcome! But this is carping. The Attain-ment Targets were designed with the aim of 'encouraging pupils to think for themselves' (1.14). Concern that school history might 'be used as propaganda; that governments of one hue or another will try to subvert it for the purpose of indoctrination or social engineering' led to the stress on 'interpretation and points of view' as one of these Targets: 'respect for evidence...historical objectivity...' and awareness of the need for constant re-examination of theories and interpretations was to help pupils to appreciate that there is 'no final answer to any historical question' and that there are 'no monopolies of truth' (3.29). As such, history 'will be a valuable training for future citizens of a democracy'. And, one might add, of global citizens.

The original *Final Report* included much that was praiseworthy in this respect. Recognising the needs of pupils in a multicultural society, it sought to 'introduce pupils to a range of their historical inheritances, some of which are shared and others individual'. It also referred to 'the continuing search for international peace'; urged that 'education in British society should be rooted in toleration and respect cultural variety'; and believed that 'studying the history of other societies from their own perspectives and for their own sakes counteracts tendencies to insularity.' However, the Report was too much for the then Prime Minister, Mrs Thatcher, and the Education Secretary, Mr John MacGregor. They wanted more than the 60% weighting offered for uniquely British history and more concentration on the 'facts' of history as against principles of interpretation and evaluation. A number of good things were lost in the revision that followed the Ministerial intervention, but to Mr MacGregor's credit it must be admitted that the revised 'official' History programme gained in clarity, simplicity and brevity. Fortunately, by avoiding a plethora of dates marking 'the great landmarks of British history' favoured by Mrs Thatcher, and by conflating a number of the study units, Commander Michael Saunders Watson, chairman of the history working group, was able to keep largely to his original objective: 'We were adamant (he said) that an official government history should be avoided at all costs.'

4.   National Curriculum History programme: revised version

'The old order changeth, yielding place to new.' In no sphere, perhaps, are Tennyson's words more true than in that of the National Curriculum, as new Orders come and go! So there is no guaranteeing that the present 'revised version' of the History programme will be current when the present text goes to press. However, teachers can no doubt operate in the spirit of the current revision even if the details should be subsequently changed. At least they will know that they have the backing of a committee of historians and educationists behind them whoever the current Secretary of State may be.

The Attainment Targets of the 'revised version' of the History programme have been reduced to three: (1) Knowledge and understanding of History; (2) Interpretations of History; and (3) Use of Historical sources. And for each of these targets ten levels of attainment are specified. The Attainment Targets concern the knowledge, skills and understandings the learners are intended to acquire, while the Programmes related to each of these targets outline the matters, skills and processes that are to be taught. Clearly the programmes cannot prescribe *limits* to what is taught (these depend upon time limits and the joint capacities of teacher and pupils); but they do prescribe the core which must legally be covered in the classroom. Some of the 'general requirements' running through all the programmes of study are of interest from the point of view of the international dimension:

— The programme of study should enable pupils to develop knowledge and understanding of British, European and world history.

— pupils should have opportunities to...explore links between history and other subjects;

— (and) develop knowledge, understanding and skills related to cross-curricular themes, in particular citizenship, environmental, health and careers education, and education for economic and industrial understanding.

It is obvious, for example, that 'economic and industrial understanding' cannot be achieved in today's world without awareness of international issues — movement of raw materials and manufactured goods from country to country; 'Third World' cash crops; multinational corporations; the World Bank, etc. — study of these brings out the interconnectedness of the world's trade, manufacturing and agricultural activities.

Objectivity is the keynote of the Attainment Targets, but there is also scope for imagination and empathy. Although the weighting of the programmes is heavily in favour of British history, the qualities to be encouraged should also be of value in respect of pupils' understanding of wider issues. For example 'show an awareness that historical events usually have more than one cause and consequence' (AT1, level 4) is a defence against brainwashing with over-simplified explanations; and 'identify different types of cause and consequence' (level 5) provides the necessary practice in developing this insight. 'Show an understanding that change and progress are not the same' (level 6) and 'describe the different ideas and attitudes of people in an historical situation' (ibid) can, in certain contexts, be considered together, revealing that what is progress for one group may simply be change (and often change for the worse) for another group. This concept has further reverberations at level 7: 'show an awareness that different people's ideas and attitudes are often related to their circumstances', and at level 8: 'Show an understanding of the diversity of people's ideas, attitudes and circumstances in complex historical situations', and at levels 9 and 10. Throughout AT1 the attainment targets require an increasing awareness of the complexity of historical events, culminating at level 10: 'show an understanding of the issues involved in describing, analysing and explaining complex historical situations', with the (non-statutory) example: 'Discuss why it is difficult to generalise about and explain the attitudes of different countries towards the League of Nations'. At level 9 an interesting example relating to 'motives' suggests: 'Present to the class an account of the causes of the Second World War, making connections between the consequences of the First World War, other general causes, and the intentions and motives of Hitler.'

Attainment Target 2 focusing on 'interpretations of history' begins advisedly at level 1 with: 'understand that stories may be about real people or fictional characters' with the example 'Recognise the difference between a fairytale and a story about the past'. It continues with insight into 'different versions' about the past (level 2) and distinguishing 'between a fact and a point of view' (level 3); recognising that

Mikhail Gorbachev

Born March 2nd 1931 in the region of Stavropol, in the southern region of the ex-USSR, Gorbachev became Secretary-General of the USSR in 1985. His application of the principles of Glasnost and Perestroika sought to combat corruption, reorganise the Soviet system and promote international peace. As a result of his policies, the collapse of the Berlin Wall in 1989 signalled an end to the Cold War between East and West and opened a new chapter in international relations. This event will become official National Curriculum 'history' in about AD2010! But, unofficially, they can scarcely be ignored.

'deficiencies in evidence may lead to different interpretations of the past' (level 4), resulting perhaps in plain error (level 5). Level 7, dealing with 'strengths and weakness of different interpretations', offers the example: 'Investigate the extent to which film or drama give accurate or complete accounts of events in the history of Germany'; and level 8, concerned with 'attitudes and circumstances' and interpretation, suggests the example: 'Comment on how far an account of the Cold War is likely to have been influenced by the background and political views of the writer'. Level 9 requires students to be able to 'explain why different groups or societies interpret and use history in different ways', offering the example:'Show how and why there have been different views of the historical importance and significance of particular figures, for example: Winston Churchill, Lenin or Eva Peron'. Such an exercise offers considerable scope for developing insight into different groups, cultures and nations.

Attainment Target 3, focusing on 'the use of historical sources', requires pupils to learn to 'form judgements about their reliability and value'. They must learn to 'make deductions from historical sources' (level 3) and to 'put together information drawn from different historical sources' (such as maps, old newspapers, photographs, etc) (level 4). Gradually the requirements are made more demanding until at level 10 they should be able to 'explain the problematic nature of historical evidence, showing an awareness that judgements based on historical sources may well be provisional'. The example suggested for this level is: 'Explain how the limitations of sources relating to the 'Cultural Revolution' make it difficult to form a complete picture of what took place in China at that time'. All this is a far cry from the simple fact-mongering and date-learning that sometimes characterised history teaching in earlier days.

Moving now to the Programmes of study, those for Key Stage 1 and 2 are essentially Eurocentric, though they are not without opportunities for incorporating a global dimension. For example, at key stage 1, 'Pupils should be helped to develop an awareness of the past through stories from different periods and cultures, including: well-known myths and legends; stories about historical events; eyewitness accounts of historical events; (and) fictional stories set in the past'. There are no specific restrictions of time or place and so, particularly perhaps in a multicultural classroom, a wide range of stories and memories would be appropriate. Similarly, teaching about 'the lives of different kinds of famous men and women, for example: rulers, saints, artists, engineers, explorers, inventors, pioneers' provides considerable scope for including non-European figures where appropriate. It is a healthy sign, moreover, that the rulers are included on equal terms with a range of people who have made equal if not greater contributions to historical developments. Elsewhere, teaching about everyday life (clothes, houses, diet, shops, jobs, transport, entertainment, etc.) provides a welcome change from the concentration on perpetual power struggles, battles and mayhem that was the stuff of school history for some of us. And in all of this, pupils are to be 'encouraged to ask questions about the past', so that they take an active and not simply a passive role in their historical education.

For Key Stage 2, in addition to 'important episodes and developments in Britain's past, from Roman to modern times' and some local history, pupils 'should be taught about ancient civilisations and the history of other parts of the world', though (it seems) largely from a Eurocentric perspective. The fact that they should be taught about 'the social, cultural, religious and ethnic diversity of the societies studied' can help to squash the myths of racial purity that still seem to emerge from time to time. There are units on the Romans, Anglo-Saxons and Vikings (Core Study Unit 1), on Tudor and Stuart times (CSU2), Victorian Britain (CSU3), Britain since 1930 (SCU4), Ancient Greece (CSU5), and Exploration and encounters 1450-1550 (CSU6), plus three or four units of a thematic nature. Obviously, teaching about 'explorers, including Drake and Raleigh, and their voyages' and 'the beginnings of the British Empire' cannot avoid discussion of slavery, its impact on Africa at the time and its implications later; and discussion of 'religious changes' provides scope for encouraging tolerance and understanding of different faiths and sects. Similarly, in the 'Britain since 1930' unit, the theme of 'immigration and emigration' can raise important issues respecting tolerance and Human Rights. The 'impact of the Second World War on Britain' is clearly an area of interest from the point of view of conflict and international insight. The unit on 'Explorations and Encounters 1450-1550' (CSU6) adopts the welcome phrase recommended by UNESCO: 'the encounter between two cultures' regarding the events of 1492 and subsequent developments. It also makes way for some study of the Aztec civilisation, though oddly the Amerindian way of life seems to have been overlooked.

The Supplementary study units provide some scope for an international dimension. For example, unit A (to be chosen from one of the themes: ships and seafarers; food and farming; houses and places of worship; writing and printing; land transport; and domestic life, families and childhood) should 'show links between local, British, European and world history'. Unit C is to involve 'the study of a past non-European society, chosen from: Ancient Egypt, Mesopotamia, Assyria,, the Indus Valley, the Maya or Benin'. The inclusion of Benin is a welcome recognition that Africa has a history of its own independent of European activity. The unit should 'involve study from a variety of perspectives: political; economic, technological and scientific; social; religious; cultural and aesthetic' as well as the 'everyday lives of men and women'. This unit, like the nineteenth century study of Classical history (except from the language point of view), will offer both the advantages and disadvantages of detachment. Where a sense of relevance may be missing, an increased element of historical objectivity will be facilitated.

All the programmes from Key Stage 2 to Key Stage 4 have the general requirements that 'pupils should be taught history from a variety of perspectives: political; economic, technological and scientific; social; religious; (and) cultural and aesthetic'. The programme for Key Stage 3 deals with 'developments from the early Middle Ages to the era of the Second World War'; the legacy of ancient Rome 'to Britain, Europe and the world'; and provides that students 'should have opportunities to study developments in Europe and the non-European world, and be helped to understand how the histories of different countries are linked'. This last element is largely to be achieved in Supplementary Unit C with its 'focus on the key historical issues concerning people of non-European background in a past society in Asia, Africa, America or Australasia'. The (non-statutory) examples suggested are: Islamic civilisation, Imperial China, India (from the Moghul Empire to the coming of the British), the civilisations of Peru, Indigenous peoples of North America and 'Black peoples of the Americas: sixteenth to early twentieth centuries'. Other possibilities could include the history of a former African culture or Japan, for example, according to the specialisms and circumstances of individual schools.

There is no need to consider the other units in detail since the general approach has been discussed in relation to the Assessment Targets. However, one or two points of particular interest from the international perspective are worth mentioning. In unit CSU2 on Medieval Britain, the study of 'the idea of Christendom and the extent to which the British Isles were part of a wider European world' is a healthy reminder that a 'Little England' mentality is a late product rather than a historic one. However, CSU5 on the era of the Second World War dealing with 'the experience and impact of war in Europe, Asia and other parts of the world' extends pupils' perspectives further in recognition that Europe cannot isolate itself from global interdependence. The unit includes attention to the role of wartime leaders, the Holocaust, the dropping of atomic bombs on Hiroshima and Nagasaki, and the 'origins of the United Nations, including the UN Charter and Universal Declaration of Human Rights' and the problems of refugees. It is good to see that these important elements are at last required to be taught in all state schools.

The programme of study for Key Stage 4, dealing with Britain, Europe and the world in the twentieth century, is also to be welcomed:

> Pupils should be taught to understand how the world in which they live has been shaped by developments in twentieth- century history. This programme of study should develop historical knowledge which will help pupils to understand the background to the modern world but it is not a course in current affairs. It should focus on events from the turn of the century to about twenty years before the present day. Pupils should be helped to consolidate their understanding of earlier periods of history. Through their historical studies they should have opportunities to prepare themselves for citizenship, work and leisure.

Whatever was the intention of the Education Secretary who decreed that history should stop twenty years ago, the spirit of the original History Working Group's *Final Report* can be preserved within the tactful rubric of their revision. There is no reason against historical study *focusing* on events up to twenty years ago, but 'focus' does not prescribe limits, and it would be the odd historian who could stop dead (metaphorically speaking) at an arbitrary line when so many exciting historical events affecting our lives and needing explanation have happened since. The 'focus' may end when Nixon was President of the USA and the United States' army was still in Vietnam; when Brezhnev ruled a Union of Soviet Socialist Republics that no longer exists; when Mrs Gandhi was Prime Minister of India and Mrs Thatcher a back-bencher in the UK; when President Obote of Uganda was deposed by Idi Amin; and so on — but important *changes, connections and implications* of events of that period would naturally need discussion. It is true that a distinction can be made between the study of 'current affairs' and the study of history: but if the exigencies of the National Curriculum should displace the current affairs sessions that used to be a feature of upper secondary school life (as well they might), and since students will have been encouraged to ask questions throughout the History programme, it is highly likely that matters beyond the strict 'focus' of study will arise. It was found during the Gulf War that the discussion of contemporary issues can help to diffuse school tension. An article in *The Independent* (26 January 1991) reported on how it helped cope with emotions roused in schools with Muslim pupils: 'The crisis does not fit neatly into the national curriculum (the correspondent wrote) but schools have seen classroom discussion as the best way to deal with questions and conflicting arguments'.

TIME CHART

Some significant dates in international relations, conflict resolution and democratic advance.

1863 International Red Cross founded in Geneva by H. Dunant

1864 First Geneva Convention to protect war victims, initiated by International Red Cross, signed 24 August by 58 governments; others followed in 1949.

1865 Slavery abolished, USA (31 January)

1899 First Hague Peace Conference: World Court established

1913 Hague Academy of International Law founded, The Hague

1920 League of Nations founded, Geneva (10 January)

1921 War Resisters International founded (16 March)

1922 CICI (International Committee on Intellectual Co-operation) founded, Geneva

1928 All women get the vote, UK (2 July)

1945 United Nations Charter, first signed by 51 nations, came into force (24 October)

1945 UNESCO constitution signed by 37 Governments in London (16 November)

1948 Universal Declaration of Human Rights by UN General Assembly (10 December)

1958 CND (Campaign for Nuclear Disarmament) launched, London (28 February)

1961 Amnesty International's first appeal launched (28 May)

1963 Partial Test Ban Treaty signed (5 August)

1967 Outer Space Treaty signed (27 January)

1968 Race Relations Bill, UK (23 April)

1969 Abolition of death penalty, UK (18 December)

1971 Sea-bed Treaty signed (11 February)

1975 Biological Weapons Convention (26 March)

1982 Nuclear Non-Proliferation Treaty signed (5 March)

1985 Unilateral Moratorium on Nuclear Tests, USSR (6 August)

1986 Gorbachev in the Far East defines *Perestroika*: 'a new revolution'

1987 Independent journal *Glasnost* founded in Russia (July)

1989 Berlin Wall down (10 November) signalling end of the Cold War

To attempt to outline the items in the Key Stage 4 programme that have an international dimension would involve quoting the greater part of it, and so it seems better to refer the reader to the document itself. Apart from the fact that its coverage is so wide that it may well be difficult to organise in the time available, it seems to me to be an excellent programme. Its spirit and orientation are sound, and there can be little doubt that the citizens it is seeking to prepare are 'world citizens'. The world these citizens will inherit is in some important respects very different from what it was twenty years ago.

Perestroika, as originally conceived by Gorbachev has come to an end, since the Communism it was meant to reform and restructure has collapsed; but while the concept was in vogue it performed a valuable task in shaking off fixed and unproductive habits of thought and action. *Glasnost*, on the other hand, has permanent work to do: 'openness' and freedom to express one's ideas and beliefs are essential elements of democracy. Authoritarian systems, which put the interests of the State above the interests of the individual lives that comprise it, cannot abide openness. They have to ensure that the education delivered to their youth is rigidly conformist. Democratic systems, on the other hand, ask a lot of their citizens in terms of personal responsibility and imaginative participation. They therefore need to provide an education which is flexible, creative and open. Within limits, the History programme of the National Curriculum has gone at least some way towards achieving this.

Education should *empower* pupils with a sense of control over their own lives and of a capacity to influence events. This means encouraging independent thinking. As Eric Fromm wrote in *The Fear of Freedom* (1942): 'The right to express our thoughts...means something only if we are able to have thoughts of our own to express'. Fromm also warns us against 'the pathetic superstition that by knowing more and more facts one arrives at knowledge of reality'. He echoes the thinking of the History Working Group when he writes,

> To be sure, thinking without a knowledge of facts remains empty and fictitious; but 'information' alone can be just as much an obstacle to thinking as a lack of it. (p.214)

Mugging up facts wholesale consumes the energy that should be given to achieving real understanding. Original thinking, however, can also be discouraged by regarding 'all truth as relative...an entirely subjective matter, almost a matter of taste'. This is a potential danger in the 'alternative interpretations' approach to history teaching and the 'balance' teachers are always being asked to strike. Some things matter more than others, and some views are better than others. Teachers need somehow to convey this without being propagandist in their teaching. Finally, pupils should be encouraged not to be intimidated by the 'kind of smokescreen...that the problems are too difficult for the average individual to grasp' (Fromm, 1942). The 'leave-it-to-the-experts' mentality has endangered our environment globally almost to the point of no return. By encouraging spontaneous, creative activity in pupils we can help them develop the confidence requisite for democratic world citizens of the twenty-first century.

Chapter 3

The Core Subjects (1) English

Language is an arbitrary and conventional vocal system of symbols by means of which human being communicate and co-operate with one another. (Simeon Potter)

In the school curriculum English is unique: the child begins to acquire language before school, without it no other process of thought and study can take place, and it continues to be central throughout life.
(The Kingman Report, 1988)

...language can be a bond between members of a group, a symbol of national pride, a barrier and a source of misunderstandings, and can be used to alienate, insult, wound, offend, praise or flatter, be polite or rude.
(The National Curriculum, 1990)

English Language in the National Curriculum

English is a broad subject, and in order to deal adequately with it a somewhat arbitrary division has had to be made. This chapter, therefore, deals with one aspect of English in the National Curriculum — English as 'language'; its other main aspect, 'literature', is reserved for Chapters 8 and 9. We look first at language as *communication*, then at language mastery for the *individual*, then at language for *discrimination*, and finally the use of language for *writing*.

1. Communication

The English programme in the National Curriculum could have taken a number of forms. Fortunately the English Working Group, under Professor Brian Cox, created a programme which provided teachers with valuable guidelines while encouraging them to adopt creative and progressive approaches to their work. The emphases — based on familiar good practice among English teachers and many others — will be welcomed by teachers concerned with international understanding and conflict resolution. Since this original programme was published a new committee under the chairmanship of David Pascall has produced revised proposals which are likely to come into force during 1994 and 1995. These, however, 'do not constitute a new model of English teaching' but in general endorse the former committee's objectives. The function of the new proposals is essentially to clarify details of the original programme; to reduce by rearrangement the number of Attainment Targets from five to three; and to generally simplify the presentation. Two principal changes are: to specify aspects of grammar to be taught in order to promote wider understanding of Standard English, and to provide examples of recommended literature for study in schools.

In both the original and the revised programme the co-operative aspects of language feature strongly. To begin with Attainment Target One: Speaking and Listening, this programme explicitly requires that pupils should be encouraged:

— to listen carefully and respond in discussion

— to work in groups of different sizes

— to listen to others' reactions

— to reflect, respond to or extend the ideas and opinions of a previous speaker

Reprinted with permission from the London Educational Reviews

— to draw other people into the talk and ensure that all views are given a fair hearing

— to deal politely with opposing points of view

— to negotiate consensus

Such skills incorporated in the programme from the earliest stages embody values that are vital to the development of social awareness and basic to inter-group and international understanding.

We tend to take 'listening' for granted, but 'creative listening' involves empathy, and while it makes more demands on us it is more rewarding. In her book *Let's Co-operate*, Mildred Masheder (1986) asks 'How many of us experience real active listening? We are generally half listening and already formulating in our minds what we are going to. say next'. Individuals tend to be afraid that 'someone else will break in and the opportunity to express one's own ideas is lost'. She also draws attention to the fact that the teacher's example is important. How often do we fail to listen carefully to what children have to tell us? Her book provides a number of games to encourage creative listening. Prutzman and others (1978), in *The Friendly Classroom for a Small Planet* also offer a variety of activities with the same objective. 'The Telephone Game' (also known as 'Whispers') can provide a challenge to co-operation if the *reasons* for the original message becoming garbled are discussed and successive attempts to improve the communication are made. Another activity, 'Cooper Says', is based on 'Simon Says' (or O'Grady says) but instead of making participants 'out' when they fail, concentrates on the group achieving, for example, ten successive occasions when the directions are followed accurately by everyone. The chapter 'Do You Hear Me?' concentrates on communication activities, reminding us that 'conflict and violence occur frequently when there is lack of communication. It is difficult to deal with a problem if you do not understand it, and it is hard to understand it, if you are unable to listen to what people are saying'.

The same two books provide a range of ideas for promoting participation and co-operation, many of which are particularly appropriate for use in the English Programme, especially for the younger age-groups. Mildred Masheder makes the important observation that:

> ... participants should feel free to be able to disagree; so often it is not a question of right or wrong, it is often the case that people see things differently. Children (like so many adults) tend to think in terms of opposites and the experience of many different points of view is vital to their understanding.

The danger of thinking principally in terms of opposites was termed 'two-valued orientation' by the semanticist Korzybski (1933) and it is dealt with interestingly by Hayakawa (1965) in his book *Language in Thought and Action*, subtitled 'How men use words and words use men' (sic). He points out how even the apparently innocuous expression 'We must listen to both sides of the question' embodies the assumption that there *are* only two sides to the question, and ignores the possibility of a multivalued situation. He defines the 'two-valued orientation' as 'the proneness to divide the world into two opposing forces — 'right' versus 'wrong', 'good' versus 'evil' — and to ignore or deny the existence of any middle ground'. He notes that a two-party political system tends to encourage 'two-valued' thinking, but worse still — in Nazi Germany, for example — 'Under the one-party system, the two-valued orientation, in its most primitive form, becomes the official national outlook'. He quotes a number of examples from Nazi literature, such as Hitler's: 'Everyone in Germany is a National Socialist — the few outside the party are either lunatics or idiots'. Or, of course, Jews:

> There is no place for Heinrich Heine in any collection of works of German poets... (according to the Nazi periodical *Schwarze Korps*)... When we reject Heine, it is not because we consider every line he wrote bad. The decisive factor is that this man was a Jew. Therefore, there is no place for him in German literature.

Two-valued propaganda, says Hayakawa, reduces our capacity for objective, rational thinking; and in doing so, enables 'people to do in cold blood things that they could otherwise do only in the heat of passion'. The implications of this for interpersonal, intercommunal and international relations are clearly worth consideration.

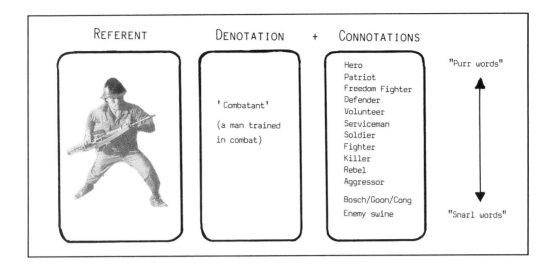

REFERENT	DENOTATION	+	CONNOTATIONS	
	'Combatant' (a man trained in combat)		Hero Patriot Freedom Fighter Defender Volunteer Serviceman Soldier Fighter Killer Rebel Aggressor Bosch/Goon/Cong Enemy swine	"Purr words" ↕ "Snarl words"

Bias in the language of war

To return to the classroom, however, and (in the words of the first draft of the National Curriculum), to 'coping constructively with different points of view', the task of helping pupils acquire 'the ability to voice disagreement courteously' falls to the teacher. Obviously, the teacher's example is of primary importance. Teachers who 'put down' children continually must expect their pupils to do the same to each other. Those who treat even their pupils' mistakes with serious attention, and *discuss* points of disagreement rather than dismiss them will hopefully find their own courtesy imitated in the classroom. 'You're wrong!', 'Don't be silly!', 'What rubbish!' give place to: 'It seems to me...', 'That's possible, but...', 'When I tried it...', 'Maybe we should look at this in a wider context...' accompanied by body-language suggestive of empathy rather than confrontation. Expressions like 'Well, it all depends what you mean by ...' need to be learned fairly early in life — ideally in the middle school years. Definition is, of course, an important aspect of semantics, and a vital first step in much problem-solving and conflict resolution. The National Curriculum does well to draw attention to the need for this sort of thing to be taught (or at least 'caught') in the classroom. How many adults are incapable of disagreeing without rudeness or hostility; and how much conflict in the world stems from this incapacity!

'Negotiating consensus', another far-sighted requirement, is not a skill easily acquired. If it were, the world would be a very different place. It is not simply a matter of debating and coming to a decision by voting. Valuable as this more common democratic procedure is, it almost invariably leaves some people dissatisfied with the outcome — any proportion of the group from 1% to 49% may bear a grudge against an otherwise fairly achieved democratic decision. To reach a genuine consensus the individual ego of each member of the group must be kept in check in favour of achieving some benefit for the group as a whole. Point- scoring against opposing points of view is out of the question; listening is at a premium, as is the calm consideration of all the relevant pros and cons of the situation. The chairperson or group leader — whether it is the teacher or a member of the class — has a considerable responsibility to encourage full and open discussion of the various points of view and to draw the procedure to a conclusion at the psychological moment when general agreement is at its height. Too short a discussion leaves quieter participants without involvement; too long a discussion leads to boredom. The Quaker practice of a brief period of silence before and after a meeting when important group decisions have to be taken helps to reduce egocentric contributions, and in certain circumstances may prove useful in classroom situations. Also, the idea of including a minority view in any final decision or statement can help to avoid leaving one or more members of the group 'out in the cold'. The wider implications of consensus-achievement can be pointed out to pupils, as appropriate to their level of maturity. If the necessary measure of compromise could be reached in Northern Ireland, for example, or Sri Lanka, Somalia, the countries of the ex-USSR, Israel and Palestine etc, how much unnecessary bloodshed, unhappiness and waste could be avoided.

Attention to a number of the considerations already mentioned can contribute to the collaborative planning of activities advocated in the English programme. As it is required that some of these activities should be 'cross-curricular', opportunities can be taken for exploring historical and geographical issues relating to inter-cultural and international understanding. Role-play and drama clearly have a place here, with scope for developing pupils' powers of empathy and creative problem-solving. At Key Stage 2 role-play is likely to be mostly about conflicts and issues close to the children's daily lives and experience (bullying, unfairness, care of the local environment, etc.); but at Key Stages 3-4 pupils are required to discuss increasingly complex issues and to learn to express and justify feelings, opinions and viewpoints with increasing sophistication. Given access to the necessary source materials, issues relating to Human Rights, colonialism, racism and prejudice, development and overseas aid, etc, can be explored through drama and role-play.

2.   Individual language-mastery

Since the acquisition of a positive self-image is a vital first step towards a capacity for adopting a positive and tolerant attitude towards others, it is well that the English programme lays emphasis on developing the independence and confidence of pupils. Language-mastery is an important key to self-discovery, self-control and self-affirmation. In the words of Frank Whitehead (1965), 'a peculiarly intimate relationship...exists between the individual human being and his mother tongue':

> ...a child's acquisition of his native language is inseparably inter-twined with his developing consciousness of the world in which he is growing up, with his control of his inner phantasies and the feelings they give rise to, and with the possession of the values by which he will live his life in the civilisation he forms a part of.

This raises an issue which, in a multicultural society, is not perhaps sufficiently addressed in the National Curriculum. The revised proposals lay particular emphasis on the acquisition of Standard English. Although I agree with the importance of helping pupils to attain mastery of received Standard English if we are not to 'sell them short' in the world where they have to compete, or at least co-operate, in order to achieve their livelihood, I don't think the English programme takes sufficient account of the vital role played by the 'mother tongue' if the pupil's first or 'home' language does not happen to be English. In such circumstances, the acquisition of Urdu, or Creole, or Chinese (for example) should at least run parallel with, and will partially be a stepping stone towards, their acquisition of Standard English. The English programme rightly urges respect for individual dialects and languages, but fails I think to take full account of their importance — except in relation to Welsh. 'The development of English and Welsh should be seen as mutually supportive', says the schedule for Wales, 'and this may require modification of the teaching within the programmes of study at key stage 2'. But no such modifications are suggested for the mutual support of other first languages and Standard English. This is an area, therefore, in which teachers will need to exercise particular sensitivity beyond the specific requirements of the English programme.

Referring to the acquisition of writing, the original programme referred to 'those whose parents are literate in a language other than English', noting that they:

may have observed writing in their own first language, for which there may be a different writing system. Such awareness of writing in any form can help pupils to understand some of the functions of written language and should be used to promote their understanding of the functions of the English writing system.

This was good as far as it went. It is obviously important that children should understand that the Roman alphabet and system of writing are not the only ones in use in the world. However, the reference to 'other' systems simply as a bridge to 'their understanding of the functions of the English writing system' did little to affirm and validate the parental language in the eyes of the child and his or her peers. It seems a wasted opportunity not to recognise these alternative systems as a resource and to encourage an appreciation of different writing systems as a step towards intercultural and international understanding. Obviously one would not want to confuse young children with trying to make them learn each others' writing systems, but appreciation does not need to go so far. Once pupils have achieved a firm grasp of the English writing system, an occasional 'once off' lesson experimenting with (say) some Chinese characters, Japanese hiragana, or Arabic script can add a new dimension to their understanding of the nature of communication and raise their respect for those who can handle these alternative codes with ease. Upper junior and lower secondary pupils love codes, and I have often found them fascinated by an elementary introduction to Braille — a semi-international writing system for the blind — or with a simple introduction to some basic Chinese characters. It seems a pity that the revised proposals omit even the tenuous suggestion made in the original programme. However, this doesn't mean that the enterprising teacher cannot offer insights into the existence of alternative writing systems should the occasion arise.

The programme must be commended for seeking to promote individual self-confidence through activities directed to encourage pupils to 'articulate personal feelings', to 'pursue an independent line of enquiry', to adopt a problem-solving approach both individually and in groups of different size, and so on. Again, the books by Masheder (1986) and Prutzman (1978) already referred to provide numerous suggestions for creating a classroom where 'positive-identity. affirmation and good self-concept' can be nurtured, particularly in the younger age-range.

3. Language and Discrimination

To use language for purposes of discrimination we need to be discriminating about language and have some understanding of how it functions. How much knowledge *about* language does a school pupil need? Certainly not, in my view, as much as the grammar school in my early days of teaching tried to cram into the heads of resistant adolescents. But more, I am convinced, than fashion has dictated for the last two or three decades. The original English programme was a little coy in this area. At level 6 pupils were required to 'show awareness of grammatical differences between spoken Standard English and non-Standard variety', and by level 8 they were to be able to 'make an assured and selective use of a wide range of grammatical constructions, which are appropriate for topic, purpose and audience'; but the steps towards achieving these capacities which must be taken during the earlier stages were not easily discovered. To use a dictionary of one's own language, let alone a foreign language, with discrimination, it is necessary to know the eight parts of speech. And to argue coherently one needs at least an elementary grasp of syntax and a flexible vocabulary. Fortunately, the revised proposals spell out clearly the stages at which the necessary grammatical and lexical knowledge can most appropriately be introduced; though it wisely recognises that since the 'fluency and confidence' of pupils are our prime concern, the teacher will need to exercise 'flexibility' in this area, and presumably, tact. Some specific understanding of adjectives (curiously omitted from the original programme) may help pupils grapple critically with the cloyingly descriptive advertising we are constantly subjected to; and the capacity to recognise an interjection (also omitted earlier) might help pupils interlacing every sentence with 'Right!' to know what they were doing.

Already a century ago the philologist Professor Henry Sweet recognised that:

> We do not study grammar in order to get a practical mastery of our own language, because in the nature of things we must have that mastery before we begin to study grammar at all.

And subsequent research has suggested that people learn to express themselves more through imitation of good models than by grammatical analysis and synthesis, which can even have an inhibiting effect. This was frequently the effect of the overdose of grammar inflicted on pupils in the early years of this century. But too little can be as disabling as too much, and as Michael Stubbs (1990) demonstrates in *Knowledge about Language*, a *total* ignorance of grammar can leave us at the mercy of propagandists, advertisers and others who would play on our vulnerability. This is not the place for a full discussion of precisely how much knowledge about language pupils should be offered, but simply about those aspects of language awareness that have a bearing on intercultural and international understanding or that can help pupils develop a resistance to dangerous and seductive misuse of language. Simeon Potter (1971) put the matter well:

> The pace quickens (he writes) in the race on our planet between education and catastrophe....It is therefore essential to fortify young people continually against the insidious depravity of soul-destroying slogans; to train them to be wary of all absolutes and over-simplified either-or choices; to show them how to distinguish word from thing, and how to discriminate intelligently between facts and inferences and between inferences and value-judgements; to teach them how language really works in action; and to help them to recognise and respect life's fundamental loyalties. In other words, it is essential to create and secure for present-day society a 'climate of literacy' in which alone national democracy is able to function and world order can be achieved.

Fortunately, the orientation of the English programme is generally in line with these aims. Pupils are to be encouraged to 'distinguish between fact and opinion, bias and objectivity' (Key Stages 3-4). They should also 'be taught to discuss alterative interpretations... ambiguity (and) hidden meaning, eg. the language of advertising...' and 'encouraged to reflect on the language of newspapers, television and radio'. At level 6 they should be capable of 'identifying explicit and implicit meanings' and at level 9 they should be able to 'compare surface meaning and sub-text'. Finally, the original English Programme required at level 10 that:

> Teaching...should make explicit what has been previously noted incidentally, i.e. how language can be a bond between members of a group, a symbol of national pride, a barrier and a source of misunderstandings, and can be used to alienate, insult, wound, offend, praise or flatter, be polite or rude.

At level 10 these matters — regarded as important at all stages of the curriculum — 'might be the subject of more systematic analytical and historical study'. It is unfortunate that these observations do not appear in the revised Proposals. Nevertheless, the suggestions are sufficiently interesting and important to warrant consideration by the thoughtful teacher.

Let us consider first how individual words can be used pejoratively or affirmatively. To grasp this students need to understand the concepts 'referent', 'denotation' and 'connotation'. Since a word is not a thing, but simply a means of indicating a referent and to some extent describing it, the 'colour' or connotation of the word chosen can influence our emotional reaction to the object, person or situation under discussion. For instance, words like *freedom fighter, guerrilla* or *terrorist* can all refer to the same referent according to the point of view of the speaker or writer. Similarly *expatriot/settler/immigrant* or *war of independence/mutiny/uprising* reveal and promote different attitudes about the referents concerned. It is obvious that words like *savage, nigger, half-caste, Sambo* and *native, primitive, heathen, aborigine* now have, in varying degrees, pejorative connotations. We can speak of a 'rank Tory' or a 'staunch Conservative', a 'rabid socialist' or a 'loyal Labour Party member'. In order to sharpen their awareness of these subtleties, at about level 4(+) pupils can enjoy 'conjugating' verbs as: 'I am slim', 'you are thin', 'she is skinny'; 'I am statuesque', 'you are tall', 'she is lanky'; 'I am cautious', 'you are careful', 'he is cowardly', etc. Hayakawa (1965) expressively calls the words embodying affective connotations 'snarl words' and 'purr words'. Students need help, but soon learn to recognise how these words creep insidiously into texts involving stereotyping or conflict situations.

Bias in everyday language

During the Gulf War a *Guardian* columnist (23/1/91) collected under the heading 'Mad dogs and Englishmen' a fascinating series of quotations from the British press which had all appeared during the previous week. Setting out the results in two columns he found that *we* have 'an Army, Navy and Air Force, 'Reporting guidelines' and 'Press briefings' while *they* have 'A war machine', 'Censorship' and 'Propaganda'. *We* 'Take out', 'Neutralise or decapacitate', etc, *they* 'Destroy' or 'Kill', etc. *Our* forces 'Dig in', *theirs* 'Cower in their fox-holes'. Similarly, 'lads' are contrasted with 'hordes'; 'daredevils' with 'cannon-fodder'; 'loyalty' with 'blind obedience'; 'Young knights of the sky' with 'Bastards of Baghdad', and so on. Doubtless contemporary Iraqi newspapers could compete with this display of double-standards.

Michael Stubbs (1990) shows how not only individual words, but grammatical forms, can be used subtly to convey a point of view. Quoting an article from the *Daily Mail* about the release of Nelson Mandela, entitled 'The Violent Homecoming', he shows how emphasis can be varied by use of the passive or active mood, or by stating or omitting the *actor* of an action. Note the difference between:

'Youths hurled bottles.'
'Bottles were hurled by youths.'
'Bottles were hurled.'

Similarly, emphasis can be changed by varying the positions of subject and adjunct around the verb. 'Blacks clashed with police' has a different impact from 'Police clashed with blacks'. Sentences describing the same item can be couched either positively or negatively to promote a different response; and the use or omission of pronouns (particularly 'we' or 'you') can alter the emotive emphasis. These and other devices are described in Michael Stubbs' article to which the reader is referred; here it is necessary to quote only from his conclusion that the newspaper article in question 'does not anywhere say explicitly that 'the Blacks are the cause of the violence', but the grammar expresses this message.... Alternative, rather obvious interpretations, are not proposed: for example , that the violence is caused by Whites and by the system that they have set up... The grammar of the article segregates Blacks and Whites'.

The task for teachers is to help students unravel the facts that lie under the journalistic reportage, and disentangle the 'implied sub-text'. The English programme's requirement that a 'wide range of texts' be examined in this way gives ample scope for dealing with issues of intercultural and international interest. All that has been said is not to imply that entirely objective writing is impossible to find; but it is true to say that it is extremely rare in our (or anybody else's) newspapers.

Another feature of the English programme that is to be welcomed is the interest in how language changes. During Key Stages 3 and 4 pupils 'should learn about the development of the English vocabulary' — including 'how the meanings and usage of words change over time', how 'words and parts of words are borrowed from other languages', and how and why new words are coined. The original English Programme briefly offered some 'reasons why vocabulary changes over time' which seem quite helpful: e.g. contact with other languages because of trade or political circumstances, fashion, effects of advertising, need for new euphemisms, new inventions and technology, changes in society', etc.

Nationalism of the extreme Right encourages a myth of a static society and a static language; a changing language indicates the fluid nature of society and nationhood. English is perhaps one of the most cosmopolitan languages in the world: it is open to all comers, as a brief example, such as the following passage, can show:

Mrs Smith[1] emerged from the telephone[2] kiosk[3], hurried the kids[4] across the zebra[5] crossing and into the bungalow[6], where she closed her umbrella[7], took off her mackintosh[8] and started to unpack from her basket[9] potatoes[10], oranges[11], cocoa[12], damsons[13], sago[14], currants[15] and a bedraggled bunch of dahlias[16]. She smuggled[17] out of sight the nickel[18]-plated Royal[19] Jubilee[20] cigar[21] case she had bought for her husband[22] and eyed wistfully the bottles of gin[23] and vodka[24] she had bought ready for Christmas. However, as alcohol[25] was taboo[26] to her since her operation[27], she settled down to a cup of tea[28].

The numbered words give a modest indication of the extent of the English language's borrowings from other languages, namely: 1 Anglo-Saxon, 2 Greek, 3 Turkish, 4 Danish/Swedish (Old Norse), 5 Congolese (via Italian or Portuguese), 6 Hindi, 7 Italian, 8 Gaelic (Scots or Irish), 9 Celtic, 10 Mexican, 11 Persian, 12 Portuguese, 13 from Damascus (via Latin), 14 Malay, 15 from Corinth (French, 'Raisins de Corinthe'), 16 Swedish (Dahl=botanist), 17 Dutch, 18 German, 19 French, 20 Hebrew, 21 Spanish, 22 Anglo-Saxon+Old Norse, 23 Switzerland (Geneva), 24 Russian, 25 Arabic, 26 Polynesian, 27 Latin, 28 Chinese. These are all fairly everyday words. New loans of particular significance, such as 'Glasnost' and 'Perestroika' are worthy of particular consideration, as are acronyms such as UNO, UNESCO, NATO, WHO, etc.

A discriminating study of language also involves, as the English pro-gramme requires, a recognition of the relationship between language and dialect. It must be revealing for many pupils to learn that English, along with those Indian languages stemming from Sanskrit, and Greek, German, Italian, etc, all belong to the same language family, Indo-European, and that these were originally all dialects which gradually became languages by isolation from their roots. The origin and nature of Creoles can also be considered, in the light of a deeper understanding of language evolution; and respect for their various forms and practical uses encouraged.

4.   Writing

A book could be written about the possibilities of writing to promote international understanding within the framework of the English programme of the National Curriculum, but it will be necessary to confine discussion here to a few brief suggestions.

At Key Stage 1, for instance, 'Pupils should write for a range of readers, which should include their teacher, their family, their peers and themselves'. This emphasises the social importance of writing, an aspect which rather more warmly expressed in the original Pro-gramme: 'Pupils should write individually and in groups, sharing their writing with others and discussing what thy have written, and should produce finished pieces of work for wider audiences, e.g. stories, newspapers, magazines, books, games and guides for other children.' The element of co-operation here is obviously to be wel-comed, firstly within the class, and secondly reaching out beyond the classroom to communicate with others. At Key Stage 2, they should 'write for a wider range of purposes' and for 'an extended range of audiences...including the teacher, the class, younger and older children, adults in the school or community and imagined audiences'. 'The forms in which they write should include: poetry...; stories; letters; notes; diaries; reports; instructions; dialogue and drama scripts', etc. Key Stage 3 and 4 offer similar opportunities at a deeper level of maturity.

Story-writing is obviously a wide-open category. In the early stages self-affirming writing is a natural option, and issues of friendship, conflict and conflict-resolution, justice and fair-play can be intro-duced as pupils are ready for them. Upper primary school children can be encouraged to look wider for their themes, for example to stories involving international sport, football hooliganism, aid for a natural disaster overseas, simpler issues of Human Rights or Apartheid, environmental matters such as saving endangered species, and so on. Articles for class or school magazines or newspapers can include information about countries of the Commonwealth, or about commemorative days such as United Nations Day (October 24th) or Hiroshima Remembrance Day (August 6th), etc, or biographical writing which presents opportunities to get to know about some of the humanitarian, creative promoters of peace and positive benefits to humankind in the fields of politics, medicine, the arts and technology, etc.: Pasteur, Buddha, Marie Curie, Tolstoy, Martin Luther King, Gandhi, Samuel Coleridge Taylor, Ralph J Bunche, Paul Robeson, Galileo, Einstein, St Francis of Assisi and hundreds of other international benefactors. Older pupils can write about development issues, colonialism, terrorism, the United Nations, the arms race and nuclear weapons, conscription and militarization, tolerance, intolerance and prejudice. The possibilities are almost endless

For actual contact with the wider world a variety of possibilities exist. At one primary school where I taught, we adopted a school ship, kept track of its movements around the world and wrote to the Captain and members of the crew who wrote back in turn, sent us interesting items from their travels and even on one momentous occasion arranged for the Captain to visit the school. Easier to organise, perhaps, are pen-pal exchanges between individual pupils, or a 'twinning' project on a class or school scale to develop relations through the steady exchange of writing with a school abroad.

Poetry writing is encouraged throughout the English programme. Two forms I have found very adaptable to issues of conflict, war and international understanding are the acrostic and the 'haiku'. The latter, being a Japanese form, in itself provides a link with another culture. This simple form of three lines of five, seven and five syllables in turn lends itself to the expression of brief, philosophical ideas:

Black and white closely
Together in the struggle
Past sins forgotten

> Smoke from factories
> Rises into the warm air
> Falls as pollution

His face bears the scars
Of triumphant victory
But inside he bleeds

These three 'haiku', bearing on race, the environment and war in turn were by older students. Acrostic poems use the title word to provide the initial letter of each line. The following was by a third-year secondary school boys after a lesson on Hiroshima:

H ell fire burning
I n the streets
R ound the bombed city
O f Japan
S ome two hundred thousand
H iroshiman citizens
I n the city at that
M oment were killed
A nd cremated by a wicked bomb.

After the same lesson a classmate produced the following more conventional free-verse poem:

Relative Sadness
Einstein's eyes
Were filled with tears
When he heard about Hiroshima;
Mr Tanami
Had no eyes
To show his grief.

Conclusion

It would be possible to continue to explore the English programme of the National Curriculum for openings lending themselves to the development of international themes, but perhaps enough has been said to indicate that there is no shortage of scope within the framework provided for work relating to intercultural and international understanding, conflict resolution, issues of peace and war and our shared global environment. A later chapter will consider the use and range of literature possible within the same generous framework.

Chapter 4

The Core Subjects (2) Mathematics and Science

Within the overall programme of study, the Government's intention is that there must be space to accommodate the enterprise of teachers, offering them sufficient flexibility in the choice of content to adapt what they teach to the needs of the individual pupil. (Section 2, The Act)

This chapter looks briefly at the Mathematics and Science programmes in turn and offers some suggestions as to ways in which the international dimension can be explored and developed. The enterprising specialist with a concern in this area will obviously be able to improve on these suggestions and find many more ways of adapting the statutory requirements. It should be remembered that from its inception the National Curriculum was intended to provide 'a framework not a strait-jacket' (DES, July 1987). Its 'Attainment Targets' — defined as the knowledge, skills and understanding pupils are expected to have by the end of each key stage — are to provide *objectives* for what is to be learned in each subject during that stage, but they cannot define *how* the subjects are to be taught nor deal with every detail encountered in the process. The Programmes of Study 'set out the essential ground to be covered in order to meet the objectives' — outline what *must* be taught; but leave open what *may* be taught.

While teachers will inevitably be concerned to ensure that their pupils are prepared to meet the assessment arrangements for the various attainment targets, their own horizons and their teaching style will considerably affect what their pupils take away with them. A teacher who is reasonably aware of global developments, concerned with peace and justice, conflict resolution and human rights — simply through reading appropriate newspapers and watching television news — will find plenty of opportunity to illustrate his or her teaching, in whatever subject, with relevant examples. Cross-curricular teaching, where this is appropriate, can offer additional opportunities to provide an international dimension.

A. Mathematics

The language of mathematics differs from that of everyday life, because it is essentially a rationally planned language. The languages of size have no place for private sentiment, either of the individual or of the nation. They are international languages like the binomial nomenclature of natural history. (Lancelot Hogben: Mathematics for the Million)

Mathematics provides another framework for viewing and making sense of the world, providing tools for understanding, analysing, hypothesising and predicting.... The choice of problems to investigate, the data to be collected or analysed, can highlight both global and futures issues. (David Hicks: Exploring Alternative Futures)

Mathematics is a universal language. Some would say it is the *only* truly international idiom. It is also the product of many cultures, and its achievements today rest heavily on foundations laid centuries ago in India, Greece, Egypt, the Arab world and more recently USA and Europe at large. Yet to look at the *National Curriculum,* as printed, one could be forgiven for thinking that mathematics is an all-British product — monocultural and monolithic. An earlier document, the DES Proposals (HMSO,1988) suggested that teachers of the curriculum 'could show the contribution to the development of mathematical thinking of non-European cultures', but even that publication prided itself on not including 'any 'multicultural' aspects in any of our attainment targets' for fear that these 'could confuse young children'. However, apart from the unavoidable use of the frozen terms 'Cartesian co-ordinates' and 'Pythagoras' theorem', the current version of the Mathematics curriculum provides no hint that mathematics might be a multicultural or international enterprise. Be that as it may, the failure of the Curriculum to spell out this dimension does not mean that it is impossible to introduce it. The very nature of mathematics — an impartial quest to discover and harmonise universal truths — gives it international significance, and its teaching can be considerably en-livened by the introduction of intercultural insights. The idea that a Frenchman, Rene Descartes, living three centuries ago, the Greek Pythagoras, living two and a half thousand years ago and Ahmes, the Egyptian, living some 4000 years ago were all excited by their mathematical discoveries can provide a human dimension to an otherwise relatively abstract subject.

The National Curriculum is inevitably concerned with both 'pure' and 'applied' mathematics appropriately adjusted in stages for the different levels of attainment. Insofar as it is 'pure', the aspect of mathematics as a 'universal quest' can be brought out. Whenever it is 'applied', mathematics involves, or requires, *data*; and this provides opportunities to introduce materials, facts, tables, statistics, etc, from a wide range of sources. Obviously, materials of international or cross-cultural interest can play a part here.

In the early stages (levels 1-4) there is a good deal of counting, sorting, classifying, etc, of objects; of selecting criteria, seeking answers to simple problems, constructing data sheets and frequency tables; and constructing, collecting and calculating. The manner or process — the class organisation and atmosphere — are vital at this stage. In the spirit of developing tolerance and understanding, the teacher can encourage co-operation rather than competition in the achievement of these activities. It may also be possible to include materials with inter-national relevance for some of this work. Data from Oxfam, Unicef and similar sources may be useful for problem-construction, frequency tables and so on. Foreign stamps, clearly unsuitable in some circumstances because of their possible value and obvious vulnerability, can (in the right circumstances) provide opportunities for sorting and classifying, since they lend themselves ideally to different 'sets' in terms of country, colour, denomination, shape, pictorial elements, etc. They can incidentally provide an early encour-agement to interest in wider horizons. Positive interest is the first step — though *only* the first step — towards later understanding.

Later stages (levels 5-10) require the use and creation of pie charts, graphs, databases, questionnaires, etc, and the assembly and interpre-tation of statistics. There is scope here for using data published by the United Nations and its agencies, relating to international trade, econo-mics, comparative poverty and literacy levels, the arms trade and so on. Tact is needed here. International understanding is not served by

Albert Einstein (1879-1955)

Born in Germany of Jewish parents, Einstein a mathematical physicist and the author of the theory of Relativity, was driven by the Nazis to seek asylum in America. In 1939 his warning to President Roosevelt that Germany might be able to produce the atom bomb led to the setting up of the Manhattan project and to the atom bombs on Hiroshima and Nagasaki. Appalled at the terrible results of this, Einstein devoted the rest of his life to condemning the military use of atomic energy and working for its international control. He was also actively involved in combating racism.

making pupils and students *ashamed* of their own country, as some well-meaning but partisan teaching has sometimes done in the past. Foreign affairs are a complex area of government, and simplistic anti-government criticism does scant justice to the heavy burden of responsibility involved. However, since it is the students' world which is at stake, they should be helped to understand that while mathematical *enquiry* is neutral, its *uses* are not. There are moral questions to be considered in the application of mathematics. Two of the greatest mathematicians of our era — Albert Einstein and Bertrand Russell — have testified to this. In relation to the creation of the atom bomb, Einstein said later of his contribution: 'If only I had known, I should have been a watchmaker'. And Russell was not afraid of imprisonment for his opposition to the Arms Race, the dangerous implications of which are now becoming, in retrospect, more and more evident to its erstwhile proponents. Data showing the relative economic prosperity of Japan and Germany to that of the USA, the USSR and the UK during the heavy years of the Arms Race (to which Japan and Germany were not committed) is in itself instructive, as well as facilitating a useful mathematical exercise.

The DES document *Mathematics from 5 to 16* (1988) makes a useful suggestion in relation to multiculturalism and geometry in proposing that 'Islamic art is a fertile area for the exploration of geometrical design'. The aesthetic value of mathematics is not always immediately evident to schoolchildren, and this would be one way of helping them to appreciate it: the introduction of Islamic art into the classroom, as well as providing a mathematical and aesthetic experience in itself, might be reassuring to Muslim students in an otherwise largely alien culture. When Bertrand Russell wrote that 'mathematics...possesses not only truth but supreme beauty — a beauty cold and austere like that of sculpture' he was probably thinking largely of its abstract beauty. Islamic art, on the other hand, is concrete mathematics and so has a warmth and vitality that is more readily appreciated.

Our word 'calculate' — 'to count or reckon, to think out mathematically' comes, as is well known, from the Latin word *calx* (a stone) because early reckoning was achieved concretely with the help of little stones. The Egyptian pyramid builders and land surveyors worked out how to use a carefully knotted rope to achieve a right angle. This kind of concrete example, which a semi-historical approach to mathematics teaching can provide, can be very helpful to learners on their way to acquiring more abstract insights. Through a historical approach, pupils

Bertrand Russell (1872-1970)
Mathematician and philosopher and Nobel Prize-winner for literature, Russell was deeply concerned about issues of war and peace, facing imprisonment as a member of the Committee of 100 in the 1960s. 'The pursuit of truth which is acknowledged as independent of the seeker (he wrote)... has been from the time of Thales, the ethical driving-force behind the scientific movement. (But) this does leave untouched the ethical problem arising from possible uses and abuses of invention.'

can also share something of the excitement of discovery as well as becoming aware of cultural interdependence in the mathematical enterprise. It is a far cry from the papyrus document on fractions, diameters, circumferences, etc, produced by the Egyptian scribe Ahmes over 4000 years ago, which he was able to entitle: *Rules for Enquiry into Nature and for Knowing All that Exists*, and the avowal of Newton 300 years ago: 'I seem to have been only like a boy playing on the seashore, and diverting myself in now and then finding a smoother pebble or a prettier shell than ordinary, whilst the great ocean of truth lay all undiscovered before me'. But both were connected by a universal web of mathematical activity. As Newton himself said: 'If I have seen further it is by standing on the shoulders of giants.' Who are these giants, and how can we bring home to schoolchildren their vital contributions to our current mathematical knowledge and practices?

The derivation of our numerals from Hindu and Arab mathematicians working centuries ago should be acknowledged, and particularly the 'zero' (Arabic *sifr*, Hindu *sunya* (=void)), without which the complex calculations enabling satellites to circulate in space could never have been achieved. Pupils should be aware of the *Elements* (of geometry) published by the Greek, Euclid, in 300 BC and studied and used for further vital research by the Arab mathematician, al-Khowanizoni, over 700 years before it was translated into English. In their studies of mathematics they can make a nodding acquaintance with the Greeks, Thales, Pythagoras and Archimedes, whose eruption from the bath to run naked through the streets of Syracuse shouting, '*Eureka*, I've found it!' should at least arouse a moment's interest, as well as providing proof of the potential fascination of such phenomena as displacement! They should know that the Chinese discovery of the magnetic needle was vital to the motivation and development of nautical mathematics in the age of Western exploration. (Note the use of the word 'exploration' rather than 'discovery'!) They might be made aware of the contribution of the Italian, Tantaglia, to algebra, of the Frenchman, Descartes, to co-ordinates, of the Germans, Leibniz (to differential and integral calculus) and Einstein (to relativity), and so on and so on. These are merely minimal suggestions. Lancelot Hogben's *Mathematics for the Million* (1989), Stuart Hollingdale's Makers of Mathematics (1989), John McLeish's *Numbers from Ancient Civilizations to the Computer* (1992) among other publications, will provide many more.

Sharon-Jeet Shan and Peter Bailey's *Multiple Factors* (1991) merits special mention. Sub-titled '*classroom mathematics for equality and justice*' it offers a global, non-elitist, perspective to mathematical activity and provides innumerable practical examples for teachers to use. It avoids the male, chauvinistic bias that too often permeates classroom mathematics. Non-Eurocentric illustrations from history include the reminder that, 'the first known statement of the law of gravity, later attributed to Newton, was by an Arab scientist, Ibn-al-Maytham'. Regarding the politicized, elitist aspects of mathematical research, the Brahmins of medieval India are shown to have been equally as secretive about their activities as the modern researchers concerned with the accurate targeting of nuclear devices. Illuminating statistics are offered, as well as exciting and challenging exercises with the accent on change for a more peaceful world environment.

The monthly Unesco *Courier* is generally a thematic publication; that of November 1989 featured 'A mathematical mystery tour'; the *Courier* of April 1991 featured 'Perceptions of time'. Unesco *Sources* often contains statistical data, pie-charts, graphs and so on. Such publications (among others) can stimulate interest in mathematical issues, as well as sometimes providing data for mathematical activity. Their particular value is that they include articles from a variety of cultural perspectives.

The Council for World Development Education (CWDE, 1 Catton Street, London WC1R 4AB) produces a catalogue listing a wealth of publications, fact-sheets, software, etc, including much that can be of use in mathematics teaching from the primary stage onwards. Many of the new items listed 'have been especially written to support aspects of the different National Curriculum subjects (from Key Stage 1 to 4)'. *The World Population Data Sheet 1991*, for example, provides mathematical material for Key Stages 34; the teaching pack *Can Development be Measured?* for Key Stage 4. Much CWDE material is cross-curricular: e.g. *Looking at Trees*, which includes activity for National Curriculum targets in Science, Geography, English and Technology as well as Mathematics, is aimed at Key Stage 2.

SIPRI (the Stockholm International Peace Research Institute) regularly produces publications with a great deal of statistical information lending itself to mathematical use by older pupils. Similarly, the media, particularly the more informative newspapers, frequently provide relevant data. The weekly *Education Guardian* pull-out section, for example, has recently had articles with basic statistical information on the arms race, Scottish independence, Algeria, market forces in ex-USSR countries, charities (including disaster campaigns, famine relief, etc), and so on. Judicious use of figures, charts and graphs from such sources can serve to raise awareness of international issues which might not otherwise have occurred to pupils.

Of course, it is possible to overdo anything, and the globally-minded teacher might need to exercise restraint in pursuing his or her hobby-horse. But where there is a genuine choice in selecting material for calculation it is surely better to opt for positive, life-assertive examples rather than negative, destructive ones — for tracing the

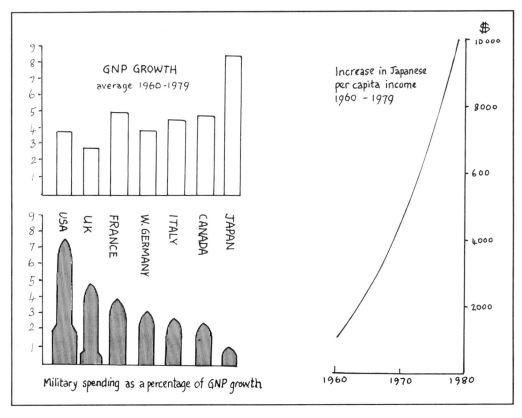

Data and Applied Mathematics

The range of data for applied mathematics is infinite: it can be trite (such as filling and emptying bath-tubs!) or significant. So it is reasonable from time to time to use data that draws attention to issues of worldwide importance.

The graphs above are based on data extracted from Chris Leeds' Peace and War (1987), left, and Derek Heater's Our World Today (1985), right. They put in question *the common assumption that military spending* stimulates *the economy to the general advantage of a country's population. The figures below (reproduced by courtesy of New Internationalist (June 1990) could produce graphs lending support to this questioning.*

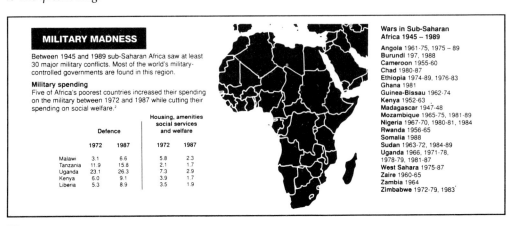

trajectory of a communications satellite, for example, rather than a nuclear warhead; or solving problems relating to the equitable distribution of global resources rather than exercises calculating the profits of competition. With, or without, a National Curriculum, choices of this nature depend upon questions of orientation and balance — an area in which the individual teacher has a high degree of autonomy.

2. Science

Pupils...should use their scientific knowledge and skills to make decisions and judgements and consider the effect of scientific and technological developments on individuals, communities, and environments. Through this study, they should begin to understand the power and the limitations of science in solving industrial, social and environmental problems and recognise the competing priorities and risks involved. (DES, Science in the National Curriculum, Key Stage 4.)

It is not the business of science to inherit the earth, but the moral imagination... without that man and beliefs and science will perish together. (Jacob Bronowski: The Ascent of Man)

The release of atom power has changed everything except our way of thinking... (Albert Enstein: Speech to National Commission of Nuclear Scientists, 1946)

The Science programme of the National Curriculum provides ample scope for developing an international dimension. It abandons the myth of science being 'value free', and requires consideration of the social and global implications of scientific developments. Moreover in stressing the openness and tentativeness of science it militates against pre-judgement and encourages tolerance and a patient waiting on evidence. A key paragraph on the Nature of Science (AT17) sets the tone:

Pupils should develop their knowledge and understanding of the ways in which scientific ideas change through time and how the nature of these ideas and the uses to which they are put are affected by the social, moral, spiritual and cultural contexts in which they are developed; in doing so, they should begin to recognise that while science is an important way of thinking about experience, it is not the only way.

On the *effects* of science a cautious note is struck in the Programme of study for key stage 3 (the early secondary school years):

(Pupils) should come to appreciate that industries require raw materials to produce beneficial products and services, and that these aspects need to be balanced against any harmful effects on the environment. They should study the effects of supply and demand and human activity in general on the exploitation of raw materials, including air and water, and on the Earth's surface.

And again:

'They should consider the benefits and drawbacks of applying scientific and technological ideas to themselves, industry, the environment and the community.'

These quotations give an indication of the *breadth, balance* and *relevance* at which the Science programme aims, each of which aspect deserves to be considered in more detail.

Breadth

To the standard areas of curricular science — biology, chemistry and physics — are added targets on the *Nature of Science* (AT3) — exploring differences in scientific thinking and the cultural impact of scientific developments, and *Exploration of Science* which is essentially a progressive introduction to scientific method. Also added are the earth sciences and astronomy: *Human influences on the earth* (AT5) considers the environmental and ecological effects of man's activity; *Earth and atmosphere* (AT9) is more traditionally concerned with weather, climate and geology; and *The Earth in space* (AT16) provides a cosmic perspective and an introduction to astronomy. Emphasis on this latter element, sensitively handled, can help to promote an awareness of the world as a relatively minute 'global village' where the recognition of our interdependence is vital to the welfare of the variety of human beings inhabiting it.

Pupils' knowledge and understanding of the diversity of life-forms is the subject-matter of AT2, *The variety of life*. The youngest pupils should 'know that there is a wide variety of living things, which includes human beings', and at level 3 they should 'be able to recognise similarities and differences among living things', including themselves. Putting similarities first, particularly in a multicultural society, can help to establish a healthy sense of 'unity in diversity'. This can be reinforced in AT3 *Processes of Life* where 'pupils should develop their knowledge and understanding of the organisation of living things and of the processes which characterise their survival and reproduction'. At level 3 they should 'know that the basic life processes: feeding, breathing, movement and behaviour, are common to human beings and the other living things they have studied' — the potential beginnings of a respect for other life forms and a recognition of ecological interdependence. There is scope for laying to rest some dangerous racist myths in teaching for AT4 *Genetics and evolution*, which seeks to promote 'understanding of variation and its genetic and environmental causes and the basic mechanisms of inheritance, selection and evolution'. The *Seville Statement on Violence* (see Appendix) can fruitfully be introduced in this area at appropriate junctures. This is a joint statement made in Seville in 1986 by a number of leading international scientists on the incorrectness of assuming violent and warlike tendencies to be a part of man's genetic inheritance. For example:

> It is scientifically incorrect to say that we have inherited a tendency to make war from our animal ancestors... (or) ...to say that war or any other violent behaviour is genetically programmed into our human nature. While genes are involved at all levels of nervous system function, they provide a developmental potential that can be actualised only in conjunction with the ecological and social environment.

The Seville Statement disposes of the idea of natural selection for aggressive behaviour, since:

> In all well-studied species, status within the group is achieved by the ability to co-operate and to fulfil social functions relevant to the structure of the group. 'Dominance' involves social bondings and affiliations; it is not simply a matter of the possession and use of superior physical power....

The Statement concludes that 'biology does not condemn humanity to war'. Thus we 'can be freed from the bondage of biological pessimism and empowered with confidence to undertake the transformative tasks ahead'. Given this orientation, teachers can look at biological issues such as the production and distribution of food on our planet rather than being preoccupied with Victorian ideas of 'nature red in tooth and claw'.

Attainment Targets 6, 7 and 8 are concerned with the chemistry of materials. *Types and uses of materials* (AT6), concentrating on careful observation and verification, offers a healthy dose of empiricism. In a world where *apriorism* and *rationalism* are too often misappropriated to support fanatical, untested 'certainties', any encouragement of sceptical humility is to be valued. Attainment Targets 7 and 8, *Making*

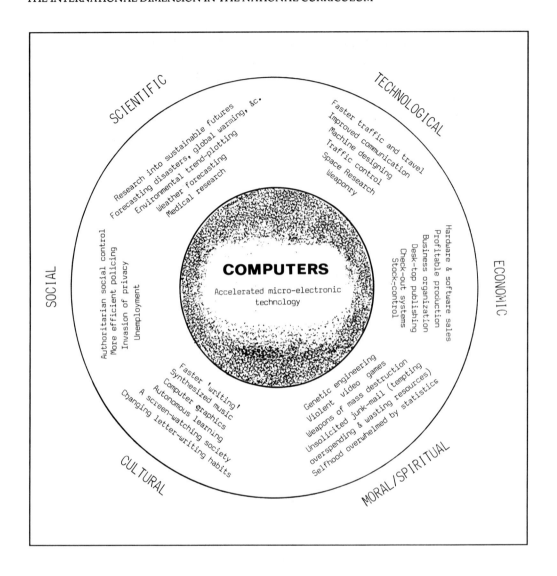

Implications of Science and Technology

Pupils 'should consider the benefits and drawbacks of applying scientific and tech-nological ideas to themselves, industry, the environment and the community' (KS3), and again, they should 'consider how far the development of a particular scientific idea or theory relates to its historical, and cultural — including spiritual and moral — context' (KS4). Since information technology and microelectronics feature in the curriculum (AT12), i have chosen this to illustrate the kind of brain-storming that can draw attention to such implications.

new materials and *Explaining how materials behave* are similarly dedicated to close observation and empirical testing, though much has necessarily to be offered as 'knowledge' rather than being left to wait to be discovered by 'exploration'. There is a limit to how much time one can spend 're-discovering the wheel'.

The remaining five Attainment Targets are devoted to Physics. *Forces* (AT10), *Electricity and Magnetism* (AT11), *Energy* (AT13), *Sound and Music* (AT14) and *Using light and electromagnetic radiation* (AT15) are in the same vein. *The scientific aspects of information technology including microelectronics* (AT12), however, will probably convey a more immediately practical aspect to young people, surrounded as they now are from birth with electronic communication devices. The significance of this field in terms of cultural cross-fertilisation, international understanding and global 'shrinkage' can scarcely be exaggerated.

Balance

There are a number of ways in which the Science Programme achieves its aim of balance. An ambivalence regarding the virtue of scientific developments has already been noted. This is reiterated in the Programme of study for Key stage 4:

> (Pupils) should use their science knowledge and skills to make decisions and judgements and consider the effect of scientific and technological developments....Through this study, they should begin to understand the power and *limitations* of science in solving industrial, social and environmental problems and recognise the competing priorities *and risks involved* (my italics).

This is a substantial move away from the innocence of Victorian and early twentieth-century optimism suggesting that, inevitably.

> When science has discovered something more
> We shall all be happier than we were before.

There is also a balance in acknowledging the range of sources of scientific developments in different times and places. In Key Stage 4, for example:

> Pupils should use a variety of secondary sources to collect and discuss ideas that have been used, historically and more recently, to explain the character and origin of the Earth, other planets, stars and the universe itself.

And again,

(they should)...consider how the development of a particular scientific idea or theory relates to its historical, and cultural — including spiritual and moral — context.

These requirements point in two interesting directions. Firstly, they echo the need identified in the Science Working Group publication *National Curriculum: Science for ages 5 to 16* (DES,1988) to recognise that science is an 'international currency' and that 'no one culture has a monopoly of scientific achievement'. Thus the achievements of ancient Egyptian, Chinese, Indian and Middle Eastern scientists (already referred to in connection with Mathematics), as well as more recent European scientists, can be spelt out where appropriate, and the importance of cross-cultural fertilisation of research and discovery highlighted. Secondly, the way in which scientific ideas have often had to battle with prejudiced established ideas and vested interest can be demonstrated. Two obvious examples to promote reflection among pupils are the story of Galileo's researches and his enforced recantation at the hands of the 'Holy' Inquisition in 16-17th Century Europe, and Darwin's theory of Evolution rejected by the ecclesiastical establishment in nineteenth-century Britain and still meeting opposition by fundamentalist groups, particularly in parts of the United States, despite the enormous amount of confirmatory evidence adduced since in its general support and the various minor modifications by which it has been amended.

Other examples of scientific achievement in the face of opposition, which might be particularly useful in multicultural classrooms where black pupils are often unaware of the host of role models available for their encouragement, can be found in *Great Negroes: past and present* (Adams, 1972) which gives accounts of numerous black Americans who have made invaluable contributions to scientific and technological research in the fields of medicine, industry, agriculture, ethnology, biology, etc. Perhaps not many people who use the expression 'the real McCoy' know that they are referring to the invention of Elijah McCoy, a black American who revolutionised the efficiency of machinery in America by means of his researches into lubrication systems. Neither is it generally known that the first successful open heart operation was performed by a black surgeon, Daniel Hale Williams, in Provident Hospital, Chicago in 1893 — before the availability of X-rays, sulfa drugs and blood transfusion. Such references are no more 'tokenism' than references to the work of Pasteur, Fleming or Faraday: it is simply a question of giving credit where credit is due.

Another area in which the Science Programme seeks to achieve balance is in giving equal weight to *content, process* and *relevance*. That is to say a certain amount of knowledge is to be provided as content; but an exploratory approach is to be encouraged as far as possible to give pupils a taste of scientific methods and processes; and the relevance of scientific discovery is also to be considered in terms of its uses and its implications. Blind acceptance of material is discouraged from the outset. At Key Stage 1 the activities should 'promote at first hand the exploration of objects and events. The children themselves should be 'promoting ideas and seeking solutions'. Again at Key Stage 2 the work should 'promote the raising and answering of questions', and still at Key Stage 4 'invention and creativity' are recommended. This raises another aspect of balance: that between individual initiative and group work. The encouragement to 'become involved in group activities' as well as in first-hand observation stipulated in Key Stage 1 finds its echo in Key Stage 4 where sixth-

Elijah McCoy (1843-1929)
Born in Canada, the son of fugitive slaves from Kentucky, Elijah McCoy became a self-taught mechanical engineer, patenting some 57 inventions including the 'drip-out' — a key device in perfecting the over-all lubrication system used in large industry today. His achievement gave rise to the expression 'the real McCoy'.

formers are 'encouraged to articulate their own ideas and work independently or contribute to group efforts', as appropriate. While on the subject of encouraging independence and dialogue in the science lesson, there is no reason why pupils' self-respect should not be enhanced by their being consulted on the rules and sanctions appropriate for the sake of their mutual security in the laboratory. If the problems are made clear to them, they may well come up with procedures which are equally as good, and possibly stricter, than those that are sometimes imposed upon them by authority without sufficient explanation. This is one way in which the process and environment of the school can help to further the ends of producing self-confident, responsible pupils.

Relevance

In the early stages of the Science Programme relevance is largely seen in terms of direct significance to the children themselves in their immediate environment. But the horizons are gradually widened, so that by Key Stage 3 pupils are required to:

> investigate practically, and by use of secondary sources, the properties of water, and the causes of its transformation from state to state, its role in the atmosphere and oceans, and on the Earth's surface as both a landscaping agent and a resource.

and,

> Through the use of a range of resource materials, pupils should survey national and global sources of energy. They should consider the importance of energy from the Sun, nuclear energy, the origin and accumulation of fossil fuels and the use of biomass as a fuel.

While water and fuel are clearly of immediate relevance to us all in our everyday lives, the breadth of reference here takes us well into the international dimension, and sensitive teaching can highlight the interdependence of humankind on a global scale. Key Stage 4 requires investigation of 'the abundance and distribution of common species, and the ways in which they are adapted to their location. They should explore the factors affecting population size, including human populations'; they should 'consider current concerns about human activity, including the exploitation of resources, the disposal of waste products on the Earth, in its oceans and atmosphere, and the effects on climate'; and 'they should have opportunities to consider the longer-term implications of the world-wide patterns of distribution and use of energy resources'. All these considerations provide opportunities to alert pupils to their future responsibilities in terms of preserving a mutually habitable planet. In addition to the population crisis, the energy crisis, the problems of pure water distribution and waste disposal referred to above, other areas of the Programme refer to the recycling of materials (AT2, level 6), ionising radiation and genetic mutation (AT4, level 8), changes in the biosphere, for example, the destruction of the ozone layer and the 'greenhouse effect' (AT5, levels 8/9), radioactivity and nuclear fission (AT8, level 8), the relation-between climatic changes and catastrophic events (AT9, level 4), earthquakes and volcanoes (level 5), communication systems, satellites and their social implications (AT12, level 8), the death of trees in European forests (AT17, level 10) and a number of other issues with obvious international relevance.

Conclusions

Clearly the Science Programme has been constructed with sensitivity and global awareness. There is interestingly no mention of dissection whether or not this is intended or accidental. On the other hand Key Stage 2 requires that children 'should develop an awareness and understanding of the necessity for sensitive collection and care of living things used as the subject of any study of the environment' and adds shortly afterwards that 'they should give attention to the welfare and protection of living material'. This is almost a Schweitzerian plea for 'reverence for life' or the Gandhian message of respect for all living things. It is not like the science I remember from my schooldays, but rather healthier. In its respect for evidence and the critical evaluation of data the Programme presents the scientific quest as a genuine search for Truth. We are not presented with 'the scientific view' so much as 'the views of scientists', open and tentative, and liable to revision; but positively dedicated in the creative support of life in an interdependent world community.

Chapter 5

The Foundation Subjects (1): Geography; Technology and a Modern Foreign Language

A. GEOGRAPHY

Increased attention should be paid to educating public opinion and the younger generation about the importance of international co-operation. (North-South...the Brandt Report, 1980)

...Geography as a foundation subject is probably the single most important vehicle for achieving an international dimension in our curricula. Whether we can meet this important challenge will depend on our success in solving some long-term problems in geographical education. (Ashley Kent and Francis Slater, 1989)

The most beautiful object I have ever seen in a photograph in all my life, is the planet Earth seen from the distance of the moon, hanging there in space, obviously alive. Although it seems at first glance to be made up of innumerable separate species of living things, on closer examination every one of its working parts, including us, is interdependently connected to all the other working parts. (Lewis Thomas, 1984)

There is almost inevitably an international 'dimension' in the study of geography, but the *quality* of that dimension depends upon a host of factors relating to the selection of themes, the areas chosen and, most important, the way it is taught. International knowledge is not necessarily the same thing as international *understanding*; and because the presentation of facts is seldom value-free, geography teaching can result in negative, just as easily as in positive, attitudes to other countries and cultures and their problems. In the words of David Hicks (1990):

> Whilst Geography has always played a major role in providing a global perspective in the curriculum, there are still questions to be asked about the *nature* of that perspective. Good world studies or development education materials are most emphatically not just about *other* places, but about the interconnectedness, the interdependence and dependency, of people and places.

These aspects inevitably bring in social, economic and political considerations that put in question the *status quo* and raise international and intercultural issues of oppression and injustice. Other important factors that help to turn international knowledge into international understanding are the development of *empathy*, the promotion of *intercultural insight* and the *reduction of ethnocentric bias, prejudice* and *stereotypes*. In addition to these kinds of conceptual knowledge, there is also a need for *locational knowledge* since world events can scarcely be followed intelligently without some idea of where they are taking place.

Fortunately, the Geography programme of the National Curriculum provides a framework in which all these elements have their place. The Attainment Targets relating to Human geography (AT4) and Environmental geography (AT5) are naturally rich in opportunities to develop themes relating to international understanding and environmental and development education; but there are also openings in AT1 (Geographical skills), AT2 (Knowledge and understanding of places) and AT3 (Physical geography). Levels 1-3 (Key Stage One) tend reasonably enough to concentrate on the local environment, although scope is offered for seven-year-olds to learn about the weather in different regions — polar, temperate, tropical desert and tropical

Opposite: The Greenhouse Effect
(Key Stage 3, AT6)

'As world population increases, so do emissions of gases because of production and consumption patterns in the industrialised countries and/or the acceleration of deforestation.' The accompying three charts on C02 emissions, rising global temperature and rising sea level are reproduced with permission from UNESCO Sources *(March 1990)>*

CARBON DIOXIDE IN THE ATMOSPHERE

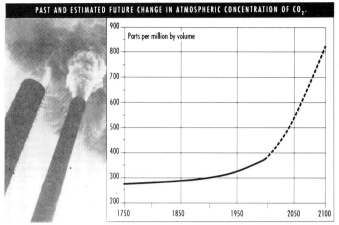

PAST AND ESTIMATED FUTURE CHANGE IN ATMOSPHERIC CONCENTRATION OF CO₂.

Parts per million by volume

This graph indicates the atmospheric concentration of carbon dioxide since the beginning of the industrial revolution, measured in parts per million by volume (ppmv). Projections through the year 2100 are based on the hypothesis (the worst) that nothing or very little will be done to limit carbon dioxide emissions contributing to the greenhouse effect.

N.B. Graphs and explanatory texts are taken from *Climate Change*, the Report of Working Group 1 of the Intergovernmental Panel on Climate Change sponsored jointly by the World Meteorological Organization (WMO) and the UN Environment Programme (UNEP).

Graphics : A. Darmon

INCREASE IN GLOBAL MEAN TEMPERATURE

Enhancement of the greenhouse effect will result in global warming, especially since the phenomenon favourizes emissions of water vapour which, in turn, intensify the effect.

This graph simulates the increase in mean temperature due to the greenhouse effect (low, best and high estimates) , using 1765 as base year.

According to these predictions, the rate of increase of global mean temperature during the next century is estimated at about 0.3°C per decade, or about 1°C above the present value by the year 2025, in other words a rate of change over 30 years which is greater than that of the last 10,000 years.

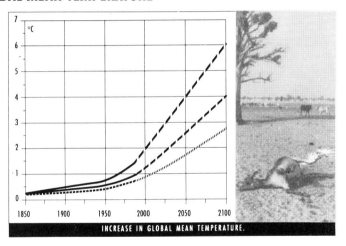

INCREASE IN GLOBAL MEAN TEMPERATURE.

GLOBAL MEAN SEA LEVEL RISE

Global warming will also cause the oceans to dilate and glaciers, particularly polar, to melt: this graph indicates a sea level rise, also using high, low and best-estimates. An average rate of global mean sea level rise of about 6 cm per decade or 60 cm by the end of the next century.

Two important remarks: at current levels of knowledge, these predictions of both temperature and sea level rise are subject to major scientific uncertainties and wide local variations; these changes may, indeed, be due largely to "natural variations". Prevention, however, is better than cure.

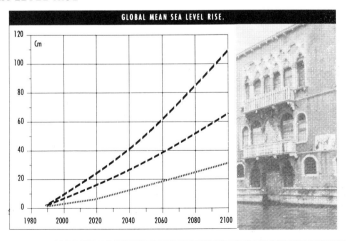

GLOBAL MEAN SEA LEVEL RISE.

forest areas. They can also consider at an elementary level 'why people change their homes' (AT4) including 'avoiding famine, war or persecution' among the reasons. Early concern for the environment is encouraged under AT5 where they can 'organise a scheme to collect waste paper for recycling' as well as 'plan and take part in the development of a school garden or nature area'.

At the upper primary stage (levels 2-5) the study of European Community countries (notably France, Germany, Italy and Spain) as well as the climatic regions already mentioned helps to extend the geographical range of knowledge; and awareness can be enlarged through a number of themes. For example, 'describe how the landscape of a locality outside the local area has been changed by human actions' (AT2, level 4b) and 'give an account of a recent or proposed change in a locality' (4c) involve considerations of economic activities ('farming, industry, quarrying, tourism', etc) and ecological issues ('the destruction of part of a rainforest, the flooding of land caused by the construction of a dam', etc) the exploration of which can help to develop geographical imagination and empathy. Similarly 'earthquakes and volcanic eruptions' (AT3, level 4d) can be considered from the human as well as the physical point of view, and the recommended use of 'newspaper reports' among other aids can bring home the immediacy of such events as and when they occur. Encouragingly, at level 4 primary school pupils are asked to 'use an atlas to find out places in the news' (AT1) which can add a degree of relevance to exercises in using the index and contents pages. It is perhaps largely through using current events reported on television and in the newspapers that primary school teachers can enlarge on the bare bones of the curriculum to promote international understanding.

In the lower secondary school the geographical range extends at Key Stage Three (levels 3-7) by adding the USA and the (ex-)USSR to the UK and EC countries; and the 'developing countries' listed (from which to choose) comprise: Bangladesh, Brazil, China, Egypt, Ghana, India, Kenya, Mexico, Nigeria, Pakistan, Peru and Venezuela. Environmental issues and problems begin to be tackled under AT2 (Knowledge and understanding of places). For example, 'describe the sources of energy in the USA, USSR and Japan' (level 6) and 'review the environmental problems arising from the development of industry in

*Opposite: **Development Issues (AT2), levels 2-10: Trade Imbalance, etc***

These charts, reproduced with permission from New Internationalist (June 1990) illustrates dramatically some of the development problems currently faced in the African continent, the most hard hit by desertification, unfair trade imbalance, etc.

CREEPING DESERT

Around 650 million square kilometres of farming land in sub-Saharan Africa have become desert in the last 50 years – and the process is accelerating. And more than 10 million people have been forced to leave home as a result of desertification.[2]

Rural populations affected by severe desertification[2]

Sahel – 27.5 million

Africa South of the Sahel – 25.0 million

Mediterranean Africa – 8.5 million

WEARY WOMEN

- Women do 75% of Africa's agricultural work and 95% of the domestic work[2]
- In Mozambique 90% of women are engaged in food production[9]
- African women do 70% of hoeing and weeding, 60% of harvesting, 50% of planting, 60% of marketing, 90% of food processing and 80% of transporting crops home and storing them.[10]

GRINDING POVERTY[4]

Of the 20 poorest countries in the world, 14 are from sub-Saharan Africa. And at least half of these have gone backwards economically since 1965.

Africa's poorest countries[3]

	Country	(place among world's poorest)	GNP per capita 1987 (in US dollars)	Average annual economic growth 1965-87
1.	Ethiopia	(1)	130	0.1%
2.	Chad	(3)	150	-2.0%
3.	Zaire	(4)	150	2.4%
4.	Malawi	(6)	160	1.4%
5.	Mozambique	(9)	170	-
6.	Tanzania	(10)	180	-4.0%
7.	Burkina Faso	(11)	190	1.6%
8.	Madagascar	(12)	210	-1.8%
9.	Mali	(13)	210	-
10	Burundi	(14)	250	1.6%
11	Zambia	(15)	250	-2.1%
12.	Niger	(16)	260	-2.2%
13.	Uganda	(17)	260	-2.7%
14.	Togo	(20)	290	0.0

PLUMMETING PRICES

The prices Africa gets for its primary products have slumped sharply in real terms during the 1980s while the prices it has to pay for goods from the West have continued to rise.

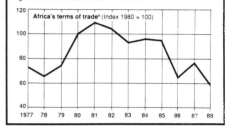

Africa's terms of trade[5] (Index 1980 = 100)

DOMINATING DEBTS

Sub-Saharan Africa's total debt increased from about 6 billion dollars in 1970 to 134 billion dollars in 1988. By 1988 the total debt was equal to the region's Gross National Product and three and a half times its export earnings.[4] Those countries with the largest debts in Black Africa are Nigeria, the Sudan and Ivory Coast[5].

This table shows the increase in Africa's total debt between 1980 and 1987[4]. Figures are in $US billion.

1980	1981	1982	1983	1984	1985	1986	1987
107.8	118.4	128.8	139.6	144.2	164.5	191.3	219.6

DESPERATE DEPENDENCE

Africa contributes only four per cent to the annual volume of world trade[4]. Yet African economies often depend heavily on the trade of a single commodity for their foreign exchange.

The following table shows those countries which depended on one agricultural commodity for 40 per cent or more of their total export earnings in 1987[1].

Country	Commodity	Percentage of export earnings
Rwanda	Coffee	69.2%
Malawi	Tobacco	64.2%
Ethiopia	Coffee	50.5%
Ghana	Cocoa	46.4%
Burundi	Coffee	41.8%
Benin	Cotton	40.5%
Gambia	Ground nuts	40%

the USA, USSR or Japan' (e.g. the 'loss of land from agriculture, removal of vegetation and destruction of natural habitats, atmosphere and water pollution'). The programme for Environmental geography (AT5) raises some related issues, such as the sources of fresh water and the control of pollution (level 4a), 'distinguishing between renewable and non-renewable resources' (4b), 'the effect on the environment of the development of (different) energy resources' (6a) and the identification of 'possible causes of environmental change' (e.g. the effect of increasing levels of carbon dioxide in the atmosphere on sea levels 'in different parts of the world' — which draws attention to issues of interdependence). Under the heading of 'patterns of trade between countries'(level 7g), where types of exports and imports between developed and developing countries are to be considered, it is suggested that students should 'review the value placed upon... commodities and services and analyse the problems caused by imbalance in value' — with clear implications regarding exploitation and injustice.

Attainment Target Two (level 7b) suggests 'identifying the characteristics of development by reference to GDP (Gross Domestic Product), value by type of exports and imports, birth rate, death rate, infant mortality, illiteracy, (and) doctors per 1000'. There is plenty here to consider in terms of international understanding. The problem is to ask the right kinds of questions about 'development'. The Brandt Commission refused to define development, but 'agreed' (among other things) that:

> the focus has to be not on machines or institutions but on people. A refusal to accept alien models unquestioningly is in fact a second phase of decolonization. We must not surrender to the idea that the whole world should copy the models of highly industrialised countries.

'Growth' should not be confused with 'development' the Brandt Commission affirmed. 'The prime objective of development is to lead to self-fulfilment and creative partnership in the use of a nation's productive forces and its full human potential'. Such issues can also be taken up under the Human geography programme (AT4). For example, 'give reasons for the ways in which land is used, how conflict can arise because of competition over the use of land, and for the location of different types of activity' (4c); 'analyse the global distribution of the population' (6a), including 'levels of industrialisation and urbanisation'; 'compare levels of economic development and welfare in different parts of the world using appropriate indicators' (6f); and 'analyse the causes and effects of a recent large-scale migration of population' (7a), raising important human issues regarding the Caribbean, Israel and South Africa, among the examples suggested.

For more advanced consideration in the upper secondary school, levels 8-10 provide opportunities both of deepening insight into issues already raised and of tackling new ones. AT1, level 8c, recommends using a database package, etc, to 'identify variations in quality of life' and brings together more variables to be interrelated. And more subtlety is introduced into questions of interdependence and international trade at level 8e where students are recommended to 'explain the extent to which shifts in the terms or balance of trade may benefit some countries and disadvantage others'; and governmental influence is added at 9c with the suggestion that students 'review the effects on trade patterns of the establishment of trading blocs; preferential trading arrangements; the use of tariffs and quotas; (and) international cartels'. The effects of 'foreign investments, loans and development assistance programmes' are raised at level 10c (AT2). In the area of physical geography some man-made problems are to be included under level 10b (AT3): 'explain how desertification in semi-arid lands may result from physical processes and human activities'. But under Human geography (AT4) positive solutions to various problems are to be explored: 'analyse the cause of uneven economic developments in and between countries and make an appraisal of actions and policies intended to redress such imbalances' (level 8c); and 'examine international strategies for improving the quality of life in economically developing countries' (10b). Among environmental issues (AT5) 'the concepts of sustainable development, stewardship and conservation' are to be examined (level 10a) and at 9a students must 'explain the implications for international co-operation of resource and environmental management' for which it is suggested that they 'describe the problems caused by water and atmospheric circulation, crossing political boundaries, deforestation, global warming, acid rain; and the need for international co-operation to solve them'.

In principle then there is a great deal of scope within the geography programme to develop positive, forward-looking attitudes to worldwide problems and possibilities. Much, however, will depend upon the textbooks available in classrooms since, although many teachers prepare a great deal of excellent material themselves, there is generally a need for published material to provide background and continuity in geography courses, and the influence of these upon attitudes can be critical.

David Hicks drew attention to text-book problems in two important studies: *Bias in Geography Textbooks* (1980) and *Images of the World: an introduction to bias in teaching materials* (1981). And more recently Gillian Klein's *Reading into Racism* (1985) provides a valuable analysis of problems of bias and racism in children's books right across the curriculum. An earlier book (now out of print), *The Slant of the Pen* (1981), edited by Roy Preiswerk, offers a helpful model for analysing how subtleties of language as well as the presentation of 'facts' and ideas can harm international and intercultural understanding by excluding, insulting or marginalizing individuals, groups or 'alien' cultures. In particular Preiswerk's book shows how racism can be affirmed (consciously or unconsciously) by (1) self-aggrandisement and idealisation of the dominant group'; (2) 'degradation or suppression of the dominated group'; and (3) 'systematic rationalisation and justification of the unequal relationship'. All of these dangers are potentially inherent in geography teaching. Let us consider them in turn.

(1) *Eurocentrism*, for example, *idealises* Western culture; sets it up as a standard by which all other cultures should be judged; ignores precolonial periods before other societies were 'discovered' by white explorers; extols scientific, technological and industrial achievements as the height of civilization and implies that white-skinned westerners are the natural leaders of mankind. The so-called 'benefits' of European colonisation to the colonised are eulogised and the liberation struggles of those who failed to appreciate the 'advantages' of subjection are ignored. (The heroic slave revolts in Africa, both in transit and in the colonies described by C.L.R. James (1980), for example, are not mentioned in Eurocentric textbooks.) The very term 'Third World' is a product of Eurocentrism. Europe and the United States, etc, are, of course, the 'First World'; the (ex-)USSR is the 'Second World'; and the 'Third World' is, as it were, the 'remnant' — 'undeveloped', or more recently 'developing', with the implicit assumption that to develop 'like the West' is 'a good thing'. Among efforts to redress the balance are the UNESCO-promoted projects which celebrated in 1992 the 500th anniversary of the so-called 'discovery' of America under the title 'The Meeting of Two Worlds'.

(2) *Demeaning language* is sometimes used, both consciously and unconsciously, to *degrade* and *marginalise* the dominated group. For example, non-Europeans may 'jabber', use a 'lingo', or at best

'dialects' rather than languages; Their 'tribes' live in 'huts' rather than homes; they have 'chiefs', not kings; they are 'lazy', 'sullen' and 'treacherous', or at best 'noble savages'. In conflict, natives are 'killed' or 'quelled', settlers are 'massacred'; the indigenous population is 'warlike' and 'hostile'! Their lands are 'unhealthy' or 'barren'. Their history is ignored, as is their point of view of events. Their heroes and heroines are mentioned only when this can in some way glorify the dominant group.

(3) *Theories of justification* finally seek to explain the inequalities between the dominant and dominated group. Social Darwinism, the survival of the fittest, a popular nineteenth century way of justifying colonial exploitation, is not completely dead yet. In popular literature of the nineteenth century ascending grades of animal life moved from the amoeba, through the dog and the horse and the orang-utan up to man — including the 'low savage' and the 'superior white Caucasian who is master of all life below him' and there are still those who, ignoring all the evidence, consider that there is something special about the White man's intellect. In the latter half of this century westerners who want to maintain a sense of elite superiority over inhabitants of the so-called 'Third World' cite poverty, famine and ignorance in 'developing countries' as evidence of western superiority. Headlines, posters and television news continually bombard us with images of 'starving Africans', 'homeless boat-people', over-populated regions devastated by floods and earthquakes; they remind us of 'Third World' illiteracy and technological 'backwardness' and call for Western 'aid' and the sending of 'advisers'.

There is, of course, no smoke without fire. There is proportionately more poverty, famine and illiteracy in 'developing countries' than in the so-called 'advanced' countries. But the causes of this have nothing to do with the 'superiority' of one group as against another. The poverty spiral is often the result of economic exploitation begun long ago (for example, by slavery, expropriation of land and the brutal imposition of 'poll taxes' throughout many the colonialized states), and continued by a global economic system in which multinationals reap excessive profits while inappropriate cash crops undermine and impoverish agricultural systems and tied 'aid' leads newly independent states further and further into debt. Arms sales bring profit to industrialised countries and devastation to the purchasers, split by rivalries often created or fomented by the colonisers during the overtly imperial era.

Famine, essentially the result of natural disasters, is in some cases exacerbated if not caused by earlier displacement of communities or the disruption of traditional life-styles. Moreover, straitened circumstances now prevailing often prohibit adequate preparation for natural disasters. The higher ratio of illiteracy in these areas arises from a variety of causes: sometimes from patterns of culture in which women's education has been traditionally devalued; sometimes from problems related to a multiplicity of dialects in a given region; and occasionally, it has been suggested, by problems created by the cultural hegemony of Western as opposed to indigenous languages. Although it is of course true that the learning of an international language, such as English or Russian, at least by the elite of a 'developing' country has clear benefits to offer in terms of communication and access to technological developments. Finally, literacy, whether in the mother tongue or a second language, requires state financing and a measure of freedom from other pressures which is currently a luxury beyond the reach of many.

Having said all this, it must be added that the so-called 'Third World' is not in any case one homogeneous entity but a variety of states and situations in which the standards of living, and of industrial, technological and cultural achievement vary enormously; and the achievements in many cases have been made in the face of awesome obstacles. The term 'achievement' here needs explanation, perhaps, since otherwise it might seem to mean 'change to correspond closer to Western ideas'. It should be clear now that we cannot rely on the industrialist's adage: 'A breakthrough a day keeps the crisis away'. In many cases it may well bring the crisis nearer. Industrialisation and advanced technology have brought many good things; but they have not brought the Millennium as it was once hoped they would. Concern to protect the natural environment from the depredations of industrial and technological development has perhaps been voiced just in time, although the hopes of the Rio Conference have not been achieved in full measure. Perhaps, while Western cities grind to a halt with congestion and Western forests succumb to acid rain, some of the so-called 'under-developed' countries will take warning that there is not just one way forward. A number of 'civilizations', carrying the seeds of their own destruction, have passed away during the long period that societies of New Guinea, of aboriginal Australia and parts of Africa have maintained their equilibrium and proved sustainable. The pressures on the resources of the environment of the exponential growth demanded by industrialised countries cannot be permanently sustained; and the current workings of world economics tend to force a rift between the labouring poor classes or nations and the ever more comfortable, but increasingly vulnerable, rich.

Richard Schwarz, writing in the *Guardian* (20/6/88) drew particular attention to the Indian situation:

> Intellectuals in India have at last begun thinking about the state of their environment. And their thoughts will reverberate well beyond the subcontinent. The facts are horrific in themselves: flood, drought, erosion and desertification — all man-made — now threaten to cancel out the progress brought about by four decades of economic development.

He writes of a search by Indians and other 'development critics in Latin America and Africa' for 'a new paradigm' to halt 'the development rat-race'. Perhaps 'intermediate technology' may help to alleviate some of the current and foreseeable problems; but at any rate it is becoming increasingly clear that 'development' *per se* is not the cure-all that it was once thought to be. Current UNESCO projects are tending to concentrate on the concept of *'sustainable* development' — which is an encouraging refinement.

The education of the coming generation must clearly address itself to these issues; and fortunately the Geography programme of the National Curriculum provides opportunities for this. In geography teaching the *process* may be more important than the product: the way it is taught, and the way attitudes are conveyed will be a crucial factor in correcting misunderstandings about relations between North, South, East and West; and if students can be helped to acquire geographical *imagination* and *empathy* this may nourish their sense of global interdependence and sustain their will to promote it.

B.   Design and Technology

Pupils' work...will involve: using a variety of methods to investigate, develop and communicate their design ideas;...(and) considering the work of other designers, including those from different times and cultures...
(Technology for ages 5-16, NCC Proposals, 1992)

...The modern world...shaped by technology...tumbles from crisis to crisis....If technology is felt to be becoming more and more inhuman, we might do well to consider whether it is possible to have something better — a technology with a human face.
(E.F.Schumacher: Small is Beautiful)

...In rich and poor countries alike, it is possible to create lifestyles and technologies on a human scale which are low-cost, sparing in their use of resources, non-violent towards nature, and, therefore, sustainable.
(George McRobie: Small is Possible)

Since today's children will be the designers and technologists of tomorrow's world, it is well that the Design and Technology programme of the National Curriculum encourages creativity, lateral thinking, open-mindedness and a sympathetic awareness of other cultures. The original programme, *Technology in the National Curriculum,* (1990), a rather rambling, but warm-hearted document, expressed the international commitment with more enthusiasm: '(pupils') activities should... reflect their growing understanding of the needs and beliefs of other people and cultures now and in the past'. Apparently the complexities of the 1990 Order made it difficult to use in practice, and so the revised version has sought to 'simplify...the number of statements of attainment and programmes of study statements *without compromising the conceptual framework of the present Order'* (my italics). It aims to 'offer schools a degree of flexibility which allows them to match tasks to the interests, needs and capabilities of their pupils'. It puts more emphasis than the earlier Order on electronic and mechanical insight, manufacturing, business and marketing, but at the same time, 'pupils should be taught... to consider moral, economic, social and environmental issues when designing'. Since the revised proposals for Technology legitimate the conceptual framework of the earlier Order, and are in any case to be interpreted 'flexibly', the following observations will include reference to the 1990 Order where appropriate.

It is not yet clear at the time of writing how much space will ultimately be made available for Design and Technology activities within the timetabling of the National Curriculum and there are further proposed revisions of the Order for Technology currently on hold. However, it is assumed that there will be cross-curricular work involving particularly art, science and mathematics. The two interrelated attainment targets are: *Designing* and *Making*, with the emphasis on making. Co-operation between pupils is to be encouraged by the requirement that they work both 'individually and in teams, taking on a variety of roles within a group'. The five strands to characterise design and technology work comprise:

— investigating, clarifying and specifying the design task;

— modelling, developing and communicating design ideas;

— planning and organising the making;

— using a variety of materials, components, tools, equipment and processes to make products safely

— testing, modifying and evaluating.

There is therefore a healthily creative, problem-solving element in the work envisaged, as well as a commitment to products of good quality. Obviously the tasks range from simple structures at Key Stage One to complex and demanding projects at the upper levels of Key Stage Four.

Schools, however, must inevitably tend to operate on a small scale in matters of design and technology, and so the 'intermediate technology' approach advocated by the late E.F.Schumacher is likely to prove a practical one to adopt as well as fulfilling an ideal which will become more and more important as scientific and technological advances increase the danger of proliferating unemployment and cultural alienation in rich and poor countries alike. In all areas of scientific and technological 'advance' the notion of 'development' *per se* is now being questioned everywhere in favour of that of *sustainable development.* Internationally the exchange of experts under Unesco auspices now relates to work on the careful management of the world's precious non-renewable resources; increased use of renewable resources such as solar power and wind power; and more attention to the specific human needs of societies. Operations on a human scale, in which individuals feel they have a recognisable and worthwhile function, is one of these needs. Schools, because of their size and limited resources, are in a good position to support and encourage such an approach. They are also well placed to experiment with solar, wind and (to some extent) water power — all cheaply available for small-scale projects.

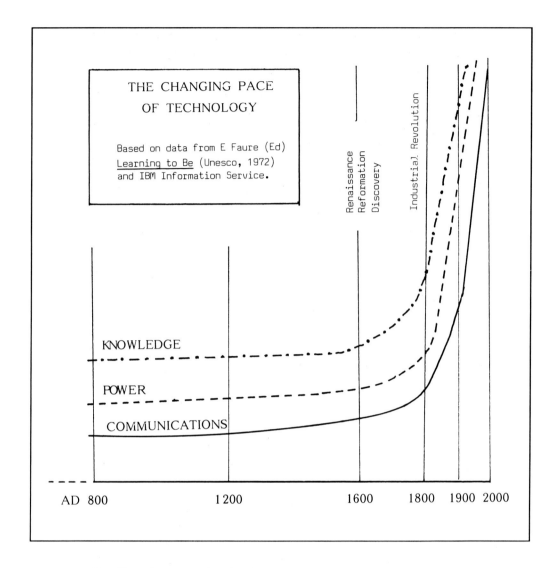

The Changing Pace of Technology

The accelerating pace of technology today creates qualitative demands in individual and social adaptability. Education must therefore provide the technological skills and philosophical attitudes to cope with constant change, and the creativity to use hoped-for increasing leisure time to advantage.

In *Small is Possible*, George McRobie (1982) advocates principles which are precisely appropriate to the National Curriculum for schools when he says: 'Let us see what can be done by relatively simple means, with mainly local materials, local labour and low-cost capital equipment — equipment which would be simple enough to be made locally.' Similarly in defining 'intermediate technology' he emphasises 'four criteria: smallness; simplicity; capital cheapness; and non-violence' as being desirable. He explains later that:

> Non-violence in this context refers to modes of production which respect ecological principles and strive to work with nature instead of attempting to force their way through natural systems.

He stresses further on that technological simplicity in no way implies scientific naivety. The best available scientific knowledge should be used in intermediate technology; but its *application* can be on a small, humanly-appropriate scale. It would seem to me that Schumacher's *Small is Beautiful* and McRobie's *Small is Possible* could usefully be adopted as the twin bibles of the Design and Technology programme of the National Curriculum.

The interests of international awareness and understanding can be served both by the *principles* of the D & T Programme and by the practical activities selected. For example, from the beginning pupils are to be encouraged to be exploratory and imaginative, and later to 'draw from information about materials, people, markets and processes and from other times and cultures to help in developing their ideas' — these are among the principles advocated in the 1990 Programme; at the same time, from the practical point of view, there is no reason why in the early stages pupils' 'use of a variety of materials and equipment to make simple things' should not be put to making African masks or Japanese origami items. The suggestion in the 1990 Programme that pupils might make 'a three-coloured batik' would ideally involve reference to Indonesian models, and elsewhere they are encouraged to look at 'Celtic patterns, Roman tiles, Islamic art, when searching for decorative patterns'. The subject-matter for 'puppets, mobiles, pop-up books', etc, or for 'producing a puppet play' can be selected from any area or culture desired and can be related to other parts of the curriculum such as geography, history, religious education, music or art. I draw these examples from the 1990 Programme, because although the revised Proposals refer in general to studying design 'from different times and cultures', no specific examples of this are included in the later publication.

Attainment Target One of the revised Proposals requires pupils to: 'identify the needs and preferences of users reflected in existing products; e.g. cultural values'. Here the new emphasis on marketing can be read between the lines. The original Programme put more stress on empathy, pupils being encouraged to 'recognise the points of view of others and consider what it is like to be in another person's situation.' And as the demands of the Programme become increasingly sophisticated at KS4 it included acknowledging 'the needs of different individuals and groups from different backgrounds when designing for their needs' and recognising 'potential conflicts between the needs of individuals and society' as well as learning to 'negotiate with people having different points of view'. It seems that economic considerations and the profit motive are coming to the fore in the revised D & T programme. However, designing and marketing saleable goods and promoting international understanding both demand a sharpened awareness of the needs of others, so there is perhaps no need to quibble over a slight change of emphasis.

The Design and Technology programme is essentially concerned with problem-solving — an important approach which militates against the educational model of 'handing down' information ready-made to students, and is a vital preparation for young people who will need to be adaptable in the fast-changing world they will inherit. At level four, they are required to 'make judgements about the moral, economic, social and environmental impact of their selected approach to their design brief' and encouraged, for example, to use 'acceptable substitutes rather than scarce natural resources', and to adopt 'a machining process which minimises dust pollution'. The 1990 programme suggested that students consider how 'in the past and in other cultures people have used design and technology to solve familiar

*Opposite: **Introduction to Solar Energy***

A pupil's first introduction to solar emergy could well be this solar cell module and minature DC motor. The photovoltaic effect uses absorbed light to energise electrons and generate electricity. Although not very powerful, the rotating motor effectively illustrates the principle of solar energy. A more elaborate system can be seen in Unesco Souces, September 1989, which shows hoe it it possible 'to supply basic social needs — water pumping and purification, domestic and public lighting, refrigeration for food preservation, dispensaries, television, small machines for craftspersons, etc. — for rural and remote areas whihc could only be linked to the electricity grid at prohibitive cost'. The article illustrates, moreover, the 'photovoltaic electricity is based on an inexhaustible power source — the sun — available everywhere — and free! The accompanying graph from the same source demonstrates the steadily decreasing cost of installing solar energy.

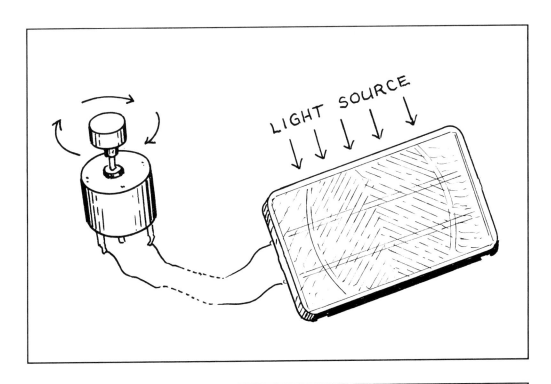

This diagram presents the probable evolution of the cost of a kilowatt/hour provided by photovoltaics compared to a conventional system (based on fossil fuels, nuclear or hydro power, plus a distribution network).

In the past decade, the cost of solar electricity has dropped from $ 50 to less than $ 5 per peak watt (unit of measurement of power cell or module under specified conditions) and, as the graph shows, solar energy is expected to become cheaper than conventional sources over the next 15 years thanks notably to technical progress which, it is hoped, will greatly decrease the cost of photovoltaics systems.

(Source : Social costs of energy consumption. Olav Hohmeyer. Springer Verlag).

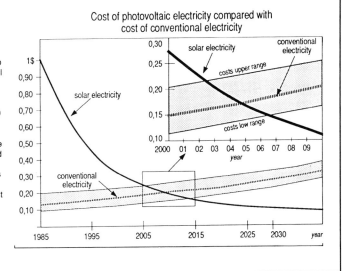

Cost of photovoltaic electricity compared with cost of conventional electricity

problems in different ways (for example in irrigating crops and getting water into their homes). This approach is still valid, of course, and helps to maintain a strong and healthy emphasis on the variety of possible approaches to a problem, discouraging rigid responses and encouraging lateral thinking. In this respect the work of Edward de Bono could be helpful. For example in *Children Solve Problems* (Penguin, 1972) young children are posed a variety of problems including one with clearly political implications: 'Show how you would stop a cat and a dog from fighting'. The resultant drawings show a fascinating range of responses involving psychological and motivational insight as well as recognition of physical constraints. Edward de Bono, incidentally, believes that

Two views of Nuclear Technology
A nuclear power plant and the atomic explosion that destoyed Hiroshima. Students who will become the technologists of the 21st Century need to consider carefully what sources of energy will serve them and their chidren best in the long term.

co-operation among the pupils is as important as creativity and so the situations he prepares are 'carefully constructed so that students can learn from each other'.

The Appendix to the 1992 Technology Proposals refers to the need for the new curriculum 'to offer equal opportunities for all pupils, regardless of gender, cultural, intellectual or social differences' and 'to respect cultural and social diversity'. However, for concrete examples of this approach we must turn to the 1990 Programme where intercultural toleration is encouraged in a number of the specific examples. For instance at level 3 it was suggested that students might be invited to 'discuss whether the preferences of others have been taken into account when making food for a festival. Have people with different needs or interests been satisfied? Have people from different cultures been considered?' At level 6 it was suggested that they 'explain the influence of religious beliefs on the demand for different food products', and at level 8 that they should 'understand how factors such as climate, religious belief and social trends influence the design of clothes'. This kind of consideration still has a place in D & T, although, of course, whether such examples promote understanding or otherwise will depend largely on the *way* in which they are presented.

Environmental issues are specifically posed at levels 3-7 (1992 Proposals) where pupils are 'to recognise renewable and non-renewable energy resources and use this knowledge when selecting materials, manufacturing processes and sources of power' and generally to 'seek ways of conserving energy'. The 1990 Programme offered a number of concrete suggestions in this area. For example, at level 7 students might 'examine the feasibility of recycling household waste commenting on prices, costs and benefits (and) competition'. At level 10 they could explore 'with reasoned arguments that although it is possible to design and make a system to monitor air pollution, decisions about reducing pollution are complex and involve social, economic, health and safety and political considerations'. And again at Key Stage 4 they might 'consider the effects of a new motorway, intensive rearing, space shuttles', etc, and 'devise alternative solutions which meet social and environmental concerns' e.g. by 'developing biodegradable or recyclable packaging'. Such issues are still relevant for discussion within the D & T Programme.

Design and technology activities can be concerned with building, manufacturing, farming, transport, water, energy, health — or even toys and games. Appropriate selection of projects can clearly provide openings for increasing environmental awareness; raising some of the human dimensions of development problems; encouraging intercultural insight; developing aesthetic appreciation crossing cultural boundaries; and giving thought to the physical or economic needs of the disadvantaged. It would be a great pity if such opportunities were missed.

C. A Modern Foreign Language

The limits of my language stand for the limits of my world.
(Ludwig Wittgenstein)

...Language is the unique expression of an historical development, of a special social awareness, and of particular ways of thought. Learning and teaching it will necessarily involve adapting to the culture and attitudes of which it is an essential facet.
(John Haycroft)

During each key stage, pupils should have regular opportunities to explore in the target language topics which deal with experiences of travelling or staying abroad; contact with speakers of the foreign language; wider international issues.
(National Curriculum)

Next to geography, the study and acquisition of a foreign language would seem to be the most obvious area of the National Curriculum designed to provide an international dimension; and from year 7 in their schooling all pupils are now required to study a language for five years up to the age of 16. This would seem to be good news. Also good news is the range of languages schools can offer: eight European Community languages and eleven non-EC languages — any of which may (given certain conditions) qualify as the foundation subject language. To quote from the Modern Foreign Languages programme of the National Curriculum: 'Schools *must* offer one or more of the official languages of the EC (Danish, Dutch, French, German, Modern Greek, Italian, Portuguese, Spanish). *Schools may in addition offer* one or more of the non-EC languages listed (Arabic, Bengali, Gujarati, Hindi, Japanese, Mandarin or Cantonese Chinese, Modern Hebrew, Panjabi, Russian, Turkish, Urdu).' Unfortunately this list does not include any African language, although Swahili, for example, an important *lingua franca*, is spoken by some 30 million people all along the East coast of the continent, and there are over 12 African states among Commonwealth countries.

Provided a school offers one mandatory EC language, any of the second list of languages can be offered for study by individuals or groups of pupils, in which case 'parental preferences about what each pupil studies from among the options provided by the school should be taken into account.' Bilingual pupils in multicultural classrooms may well be glad of the opportunity to offer a non-EC language. But for them as for all pupils 'educational and career interests' should be taken into account. 'There is no upper limit of the number of languages from the Schedule which a school may offer.' From the point of view of international and intercultural understanding this diversification of potential language study is to be welcomed. The problem of funding, however, is one that will have to be resolved: books, staffing levels and opportunities for relevant travel cost money. There can be a big gap between a theoretical choice in education and a real one. Presumably, there is nothing in theory against a school offering any additional language whatsoever, provided that the stipulation about each pupil's *foundation subject* language has been met. However, in practice, it looks as if, for the time being, anyway, languages from the African continent are to have a raw deal. The selection was no doubt based on short-term commercial considerations rather than consideration of the vast population the African continent.

There would be no advantage in going through the programme of language study point by point, but it may be worth drawing attention to some general issues.

The language-learning approach adopted is basically *functional* rather than literary. The four basic modes — listening, speaking, reading and writing — are in general to be studied for practical purposes. On the whole this is a good thing. Communication in the real world with real people for real purposes is encouraged in the programme. This is a far cry from the writing of Latin prose for a non-existent audience which was a feature of grammar school education earlier this century! Another important change is that all pupils will now be required to study a foreign language, not just a selected few. Inevitably levels of achievement will vary considerably, and it will be important for teachers to find ways of holding the interest of less able pupils. Young people forced to learn a foreign language against their will could acquire a healthy (or rather unhealthy) dislike of the language in question, and (by association) of the people who speak it — thus making the activity counter-productive.

The co-operative activities encouraged in the programme should help to counter this danger. Pupils should, for example, have regular opportunities to 'plan and carry out practical and creative activities with a partner or in a group', 'take part in language games', 'conduct surveys and other investigations in the class, school or outside', 'interview each other, adults and (where possible) native speakers', etc. They should also be encouraged to have pen friends (level 4) and possibly communicate with a linked school (level 7). Cultural awareness, begun by such contacts, should where possible be enriched by travel to the country concerned. Pupils should be helped to understand the similarities and differences between their own culture and that of the target language; and, even more important, they should learn to 'identify with the experiences and perspectives of people in these countries and communities (e.g. *in role-play or creative writing)'*. If their contacts with native speakers of the target language are to be fruitful, pupils will need to know something of the social conventions of the country or culture concerned, and so it is important that spoken language study includes attention to appropriate registers of discourse so that the normal courtesies can be observed.

The selection of materials for reading and translation can have a strong influence on a learner's views about the country of origin of the texts. Obviously, the final aim of language study is to be able to understand as far as possible all aspects of the life and thought of its speakers. However, this is a long way off for most secondary school students, and first impressions are very important. Ideally, perhaps, the material consulted in the early stages should be both interesting for the students and presenting a positive image of the speakers of the language concerned. If we cannot necessarily offer 'the *best* that has been thought and said in the world' (as Matthew Arnold would have urged), at least we can avoid the worst. There is good reason, however, in selecting 'extracts from authentic imaginative writing' to include lively and inviting texts — as well as more serious material — if the interest of young people is to be aroused.

Comics are perennially attractive material for young readers, but they are not infrequently tainted by racism, chauvinism and gratuitous violence. For young learners of French, *Orientations* selected by Richard Aplin and others (1985) is a lively pot-pourri of cartoons, *bandes dessinées*, games, puzzles and brief articles on sport, fashion, animals, detection, etc, chosen with tact and discretion. Among *bandes dessinées*, the Tom-Tom series, not to be confused with Tin-Tin, (e.g. *Tom-Tom et ses idees explosive* (Bayard Presse, 1985) and the picture-strip version of Malot's *Sans Famille* (1992) from the same press are among the many that can be recommended. A useful aid to selection is Henri Filippini's *Dictionnaire de la Bande Dessinee* (1989) an encyclopaedic guide to the whole range of comic books on the French market.

Opposite: How Foreign is aForeign Language

Students may be interested to know something of the connections between the group of languages that research indicates all had their common source in a language spoken near the borders of the Black Sea about 4000BC. They need to understand that the spread of these dialects to become separate languages is not necessarily identical with the movement of racial groups.

For teachers wishing to explore directly issues of international

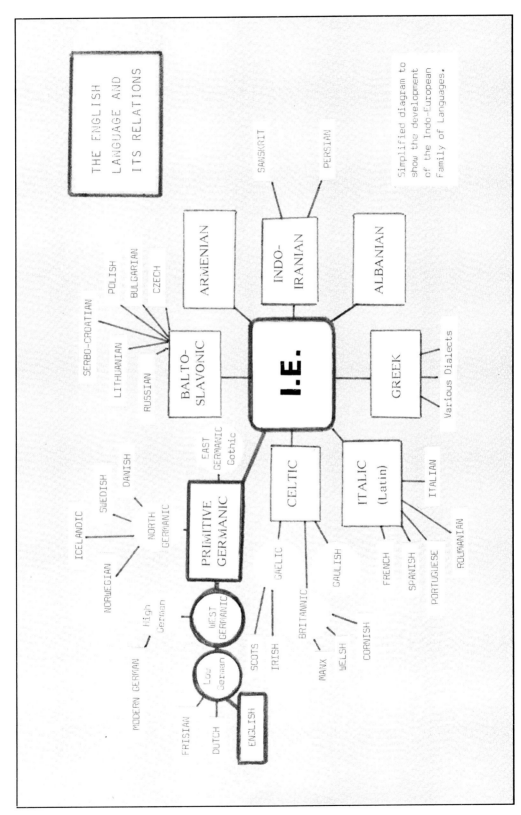

THE ENGLISH LANGUAGE AND ITS RELATIONS

Simplified diagram to show the development of the Indo-European Family of Languages.

understanding with young French language learners there are a number of relevant books available, such as J L Ducamp's *Les Droits de l'Homme racontés aux enfants* (1984), Georges Jean's *Le racisme raconté aux enfants* (1984) and Jean-Luc Moreau's *La Liberté racontée aux Enfants* (1986) all published by Editions Ouvrières, and a Unicef book *Prête-moi ta Plume...* published by Castor Poche Flammarion (1989) — a selection of forty letters to imaginary friends abroad by French children aged between seven and fifteen, all demonstrating a sense of identity overriding cultural barriers, and a concern for a more peaceful future world. Such examples relevant to the French situation can certainly be duplicated in relation to the classroom study of other languages.

The Foreign Language programme of the National Curriculum includes the reading of magazine and newspaper articles as well as short stories and novels, and the exercise of choice is specifically encouraged. For example: 'Scan a magazine for an article of interest; select a book appropriate to their own level from the class or school library, or select a passage to read from a bank of material made available by the teacher'. This puts a responsibility on the teacher to make available a worthwhile selection of material, probably in the absence of appropriate funding; but it is otherwise a welcome acknowledgement of the importance of the autonomy of individual learners pursuing their own interests.

An interesting aspect of the Foreign Language Programme is its inclusion not only of skills to learn and develop but of 'areas of experience' to be explored throughout the period of each key stage. These areas are: 'Everyday activities; personal and social life; the world around us; the world of education, training and work; the world of communications; the international world; and the world of imagination and creativity'. From our present point of view the 'international world' area is perhaps the most immediately relevant; but for developing empathy and insight into the worlds of others, which is for many one of the key aspects of foreign language learning, all of these areas of experience are of value, and the committee responsible are to be congratulated in drawing attention to the importance of this factor as a counterbalance to the danger of concentration on arid exercises in accidence and syntax.

Chapter 6

The Foundation Subjects (2): Art; Music and Physical Education

A. ART

Pupils should understand and appreciate art in a variety of genres and styles from a variety of cultures, Western and non-Western.
(National Curriculum: Draft Order for Art)

The power to understand another country does not come through politics or theories, but through artistic intuition.
 (Yanagi Soetsu, 1919)

The artist acts as a catalyst for change, provides a role model, presents a democratic way of working, provides new artistic skills, places the arts within a broader cultural context, challenges assumptions and stereotypes, provides opportunity for cross-curricular work and leaves a 'legacy' which raises further questions...
(Maggie Semple, Art Education for a Multicultural Society)

Considering the range and complexity of the visual and plastic arts, the simplicity and conciseness of the Art programme of the National Curriculum is a notable achievement. Whatever the reasons for the whittling down of the original proposals, the final form provides a valuable and manageable framework for artwork in schools. Although two major criticisms can be levelled against the programme, there is no doubt that the imaginative and committed teacher will find ample scope for developing an international dimension within the framework. But before considering some of the ways of doing this, the objections must be voiced.

First, it seems unfortunate that the statutory provisions for Art apply only to Key Stages 1 to 3. The assumption that this important area of creativity and insight has no relevance after the age of fourteen is without foundation; and the subject is devalued by being dumped at this stage. The environment of the future depends upon the quality of visual literacy of the oncoming generation. Furthermore, the likelihood of increasing leisure time as a result of future technological development gives increasing importance to the fostering of creativity. Perhaps it is a pious hope that there will be a *generalised* increase of leisure time across the population achieved by shorter working hours, time-sharing, etc, in the years to come. But whether this logical development is to be achieved or whether there will simply be a continuing increase in unemployment, the fact remains that people need creative activity to absorb and motivate them. Fewer working hours spent in productive employment mean more hours for the exercise of imagination and energy. Let us hope that the next generation will be equipped to use this positively.

Secondly, in an area as broad and open as visual art, it is surely unnecessary to stipulate that 'the Western classical tradition' should be 'at the heart of the curriculum'. Although the Orders require 'other traditions as well' to be noticed, the effect of this emphasis is to marginalise whatever is not 'Western', make it seem exotic, 'other' — 'not quite *us*', and so by implication inferior. Let us look closely at how the examples given in the Art curriculum interpret this emphasis. There are two basic Attainment Targets for each key stage: (1) investigating and making, and (2) knowledge and understanding. It is in each of the second of these ATs that schools are to consider 'our diverse artistic heritage and a variety of other artistic traditions'. When we analyse the range of examples cited to illustrate this diversity we find 32 references by name to European artists (including nine British), and the names of three American artists — making 35 in 'the Western tradition'. For all the rest, seven 'non-Western *traditions*' are mentioned, in only two of which a named artist is acknowledged: Diego Rivera (Mexico) and Hiroshige (Japan). Otherwise Indian and Japanese 'traditions' are referred to in a generalised way; as are Chinese kites, characters and scroll paintings; Egyptian hiero- glyphics; Islamic calligraphy; and Aboriginal dream maps.

By contrast, as far as Europe is concerned, the curriculum is well and truly 'internationalized'. Ten French artists are named: Monet, Pissaro, Sisley, Renoir, Degas, Claude, Rousseau, Poussin, Cezanne and Braque; four Dutch artists: Vermeer, De Hooch, Rembrandt and Van Gogh; four Italians: Leonado da Vinci, Giotto, Donatello and Michelangelo; two Spanish: Picasso and Salvador Dali; one Swiss: Giacometti; and one German: Durer. In addition, these artists are set into their cultural periods or artistic movements: Medieval, Renaiss- ance, Classical, Baroque, Romantic, Impressionism, Post-Impres- sionism, Expressionism, Abstract Expressionism, Italian Futurists, Cubism, Surrealism and Pop Art. There is nothing wrong with studying these artists and movements. Far from it. What is wrong is the Eurocentric exclusivity, the implicit judgement of all art by the standards of the 'Western Classical tradition' against which the rest of the world's art is marginalized because presumably found wanting. What, incidentally, does 'classical' mean in this context? It is clearly not used in contrast to 'romantic', since Western romantic art is included. Perhaps it is meant to mean 'of the highest class or rank' or 'chaste, refined, restrained'? (What does this imply about non-West- ern art?) This straining for cultural purity is disturbing: it's a short step from urging cultural purity to urging racial purity — and Euro- peans of my generation know where that leads.

The fact is that 'Western' art is, in any case, not pure. Bernal (1986) points out in *The Afroasaic Root of Classical Civilization* the African and Phoenician influences at the very roots of Western civilization. Later developments show more cross-fertilisation. Any serious study of medieval art reveals further Asian influences on decorative forms in the West. And subsequently individual artists as well as artistic move- ments have been inspired by non-European sources. Jagdish Gundara, in an unpublished paper (1987) to which I am much in- debted, points out how Rembrandt (1609-69) 'was not only influenced by Italian painters of the Renaissance but also by Moghul miniatures from India which he owned and copied'. Similarly, 'the architect George Dance in designing the south front of the Guildhall in 1788, incorporated Indian ideas in the scalloped arches of the windows' inspired by those of the Musjid at Jannpur. And further Regency-orientalism can be seen in 'the gardens and country residences such as the ones in Brighton and Sezincote'. Among European artists influenced by Japanese art were Edgar Degas (1837-1917), Claude Monet (1840-1926) and Toulouse Lautrec (1864- 1901). Gauguin went to Tahiti and Delacroix to Algeria for inspiration. The list could be extended. Why then this apparent fear of contamination or syncretism? For that is what the restrictive emphasis adds up to.

Cross-fertilisation, blending, reconciliation of disparate elements, or syncretism are essential features of creativity. Without the catalytic experience of exposure to new or varied approaches artistic creativity stagnates. As Gundara points out 'different art systems have fundamentally different ways of seeing, feeling and being; with their own pictorial grammar and syntax'. The attempt to understand these systems, however, presents a *challenge* to the artist, not a danger. The artist has the option of experimenting in different systems or *genres* or of seeking 'to establish a common ground between various artistic cultures'. Gundara describes how in the 7th century BC Hellenistic and Buddhist cultures were among various artistic traditions which combined to create the Gandharan art of North West India. In the resulting synthesis:

> The rich human content of the Buddhist message was the spiritual basis of (this) artistic tradition...(which) overrode the frontiers of artistic expression and revitalised local traditions which were freed of their national character. The Buddhist message of hope and peace was a powerful combination and the image of Buddha was made recognisable across vast spans of distance and time.

Later, with reference to Far Eastern art, he writes that 'The portrayal of the bamboo in Chinese art symbolises the nature of this society which bends without breaking and encapsulates tradition on the one hand and innovation on

Opposite: **Postage Stamps, Art and the National Curriculum (A)**

The Art Programme (Key Stage 2) suggestion that pupils take an interest in the design of postage stamps can have valuable repercussions elsewhere in the curriculum. Stamps are of course an international and intercultural resource and their interest can be a contributory motivation to writing to pen-friends abroad! Further value in the classroom use is illustrated opposite. (1) Various stamps draw attention to musicians and art forms; (2) stamps designed by schoolchildren (1966 and 1981); (3) the implications of runaway inflation (maths and history); (4) two views of 'discovery' (the aboriginals 'discovered' Australia some 30,000 years ago and America was probably first settled from Asia); (5) war and peace in stamps: World War I and World War II; (6) care of the environment (Italian stamps); (7) euphemisms of colonisation and exploitation (North Borneo — a 'protectorate').

the other'. It is unfortunate that our Ministers of Education cannot trust to a similar resilience of Western art.

Since the (so-called) 'Western classical tradition' is, on the face of it, the 'white tradition', it is hard to escape the conclusion that we are seeing a continuation, conscious or unconscious, of 'the long European tradition which equates Blacks with uncivilised' (Gundara, 1987). This, at least, must be the inference drawn by many British citizens whose roots are outside the 'Western classical tradition'. This, and related, problems are further discussed and developed by Madan Sarup in *Education and the Ideologies of Racism* (1991). The 'black' or South Asian artist, Allan deSouza offers a helpful perspective:

> That Britain is a multicultured society, is not only an enrichment or a diversity of experience. It is also a diversity of perception. The many peoples here enable Britain (if it would only look) to recognise itself. As much as it would seek to rule the world, the world is already here within its own borders breaking down that ruling mentality.

Art education is by its nature one of the forces most fitted to break down a mentality which is inappropriate for the twenty-first century; but it needs to be more openly conceived and all-embracing if it is to perform that task adequately.

It is highly unlikely that art teachers, of all people, will pursue their work blinkered in the way that politicians recommend! And fortunately the Art programme of the National Curriculum is so structured that there should be no difficulty in meeting the requirements of the Key Stages even if teachers transgress the parochial limits proposed. The Ministry publication *Schools Update* (Summer 1992) points out that 'Assessment is flexible, based on end-of-key-stage statements. Although there are no detailed statements of attainment and no 10 levels, there is clear progression through the key stages'. Furthermore, although 'The Orders emphasise the balance between knowledge, skills and understanding,

Opposite: **Postage Stamps, Art and the National Curriculum (B)**

(1) Sport features on many stamps particulary at times of the Olympic Games. The first two stamps point to the Greek Origins of the Olympic ideal. (2) Internationalism in stamps: encouraging pen-friends (Thailand), international Scouting (UK Jamboree). (3) Famous characters in history: Gandhi (India); Frederick Douglass (US) the runaway slave who strove for the abolition of slavery; Harriet Quimby (US) pioneer woman pilot; Eva Peron (Argentina) and Martin Luther (curiously, a French stamp for a German Protestant). (4) The United Nations and its activities. (5) International aid: the African Development Bank and support for Africa from India.

and between practical and theoretical work' the subject is seen (like music) to be 'essentially practical'. This means that the 'Investigating and Making' (Attainment Target 1) — the creative activity — is likely to be given the most classroom time. This is the area where children will 'record observations from direct experience...', 'respond to memory and imagination', 'collect images, objects and source material to stimulate and inform their work', etc. In practically all of these activities the subject matter itself is open to choice. The teacher, or pupil, can therefore say with Shakespeare:

> Why then the world's my oyster,
> Which I with sword will open.

Although in this case the tool employed will be less warlike — a pencil or brush! In fact the range of activities proposed goes well beyond sketching and painting to include pottery,montage, murals, three-dimensional modelling and photography, etc.; and the *genres* to be covered include portraiture, landscape, still life, posters, patterns and even postage stamp designing.

With memory, imagination, notebooks, collected images and objects to draw on there is no limit to the range of subject-matter available. In a multicultural classroom many children will bring with them memories and experiences (first and second-hand), as well as know-ledge and values which can broaden the class's perspective beyond the mainstream culture. And in any classroom, whether itself multi-cultural or not, teacher and pupils together can explore global, conflict and human rights issues in their creative work. Among specific sug-gestions included in the art programme are 'drawings of people wear-ing traditional costumes at special events or festivals'; 'make a sequence of images to illustrate an incident described in a local news-paper' (though it need not be 'local'); 'collect illustrations and descrip-tions from books about endangered species...(and)...make a visual presentation' (a project with environmental implications); 'note the different ways in which the flower motif is used in textiles from a variety of cultures and times'; 'design and print a poster to make people aware of an issue of public concern...'; 'discuss and compare the various ways in which artists have represented journeys; Chinese scroll paintings, Aboriginal dream maps...'; 'recognise and value representations of similar forms in different cultures, e.g. the kite in Chinese, Japanese, Indian and European traditions; compare the wall paintings of muralists working in different cultures...'; 'compare the ways that letters and symbols have been used to convey information and ideas in graphic forms in different cultures, e.g. Egyptian hieroglyphics, Islamic calligraphy, Chinese characters. Bauhaus designers', and so on. All these (non-statutory) examples can be used or adapted to bring an international dimension into the artwork, as can the statutory requirement of Key Stage 3: 'recognise the diverse ways that artists working in different cultures view and represent the world' (AT2(i)).

Obviously, issues of international importance such as natural disasters, warfare, segregation and other forms of social and political injustice, etc, can be the subject-matter of artwork; portraits can be of one another or (based on photographs,etc) of famous men or women who have contributed or are contributing to human betterment; posters can be about matters of global concern, and so on.

Part of the Knowledge and Understanding Attainment Target at Key Stage One requires that pupils should 'recognise different kinds of art, present and past, including the work of painters, printmakers, sculptors, potters, designers and photographers'; and the example suggested in relation to this purpose is that they should 'visit a museum and talk about the artefacts used for a variety of occasions and purposes'. This is an excellent idea, but the way in which it is approached is important. A museum visit, undertaken thoughtlessly, can emphasise the exotic aspect, the 'otherness', of various exhibits, and demean them by comparison with the achievements of 'civilization'. It must be remembered that some of our museums exhibit a substantial collection of 'booty' acquired from colonial conquest and exploitation, and the contrasting displays offered — whether intentionally or not — are reminiscent of the triumphal celebrations of the Roman Empire. Fortunately, the curators of our museums are becoming sensitive to this danger now and their staff are often ready to co-operate with schools in such a way as to provide an enriching experience in which the exhibits are understood and appreciated from the point of view of the culture from which they derive.

A good example of this kind of work is the ACE Project in which the British Museum, the Museum of Mankind and the London Institute of Education co-operate with schools' art teaching. In May 1991 an exhibition of pastels and silk batiks by junior and infant children showed the sensitive and painstaking work achieved in response to a carefully organised experience with Bangladeshi rickshaws provided by the Museum of Mankind, and tutored by staff of Indian origin who were able to explain the background thoroughly and help children dress up appropriately and experience using and closely examining the rickshaws. In February 1992 an exhibition of similarly high standards was achieved by upper junior schoolchildren in response to Japanese Kamakura sculptures; and in May 1992 both primary school children and 'A' Level Art and Design students produced an exhibition of silk batiks and watercolour painting in response to a Nihonga exhibition in the Japanese Galleries of the British Museum. Another project worth knowing about in respect of this kind of in-depth work is the AEMS organisation (Arts Education for a Multicultural Society) in which Black artists are prepared to work with teachers and students to overcome the problems of Eurocentrism and racism in our society. Involvement with initiatives of this kind can help to bring out the best in what is fortunately a very flexible National Curriculum programme for Art.

B. MUSIC

The prime object of music is to involve as many people in music-making as possible, not to produce university music students. (Hilary Davan Wetton, letter to *The Guardian*)

Pupils should...listen to, respond to and talk about live and recorded music from a variety of styles, times and cultures, including their own and others' compositions and improvisations. (National Curriculum, Music programme AT2)

Music creates order out of chaos; for rhythm imposes unanimity upon the divergent, melody imposes continuity upon the disjointed, and harmony imposes compatibility upon the incongruous. (Yehudi Menuhin)

The Music programme of the National Curriculum, like the Art programme, is a model of brevity. At the same time it offers considerable help and scope to the teacher. Regrettably however, like the requirements for Art, the programme for Music only covers three Key stages, being dropped from the curriculum at age fourteen. And, again, it suffers from a degree of Eurocentricity.

There is no doubt that young people will go on listening to music, dancing to it, and in many cases making music vocally or instrumentally after the age of fourteen whether it is in the school curriculum or not. The sale of musical cassettes, guitars and inexpensive keyboards is proof of the popularity of music with teenagers, as is their attendance at 'pop' concerts and gigs and their loyalty to local and national groups. But all the same it seems a pity that they cannot continue their musical development in school up to leaving age, except in exceptional cases.

The Eurocentricity is evident in the Secretary of State's view 'that there should be a clearer emphasis than in the original proposals on the acquisition of knowledge about the history of music and on the Western cultural tradition'. And this emphasis is marked in the non-statutory examples provided in the schedule: twenty European composers are named — Saint Saens, Debussy (French); Tchaikowsky, Mussorgsky, Stravinsky (Russian); Bach, Beethoven, Wagner (German); Haydn, Mozart, Schubert, Mahler (Austrian); Monteverdi, Verdi (Italian); and from the United Kingdom: Tallis, Elgar, Britten, Vaughan Williams, Tippett, and William Walton. With four Americans, Aaron Copland, Scott Joplin, Fats Waller and Duke Ellington (and two of the Beatles) as the only other named musicians, there is scarcely a balance struck between mainstream 'classical' music and 'popular' music or 'music from other cultures'.

Duke Ellington
Born in 1899, one of the many distinguished black jazz musicians whose compositions are known worldwide. His name features among those listed in the Music programme of the National Curriculum.

I have no objections to the list offered except for its obvious one-sidedness. What about George Gershwin, Oscar Peterson, Louis Armstrong, and Count Basie to help strike a balance? Or, from another point of view, it might have been useful to include Samuel Coleridge Taylor among the mainstream composers simply as a reminder that Black people can make and enjoy classical music too. In a multicultural society such cultural cross-references (even at the risk of the charge of tokenism) can be useful devices against stereotyping. In inner-city circles I have heard 'musical education' described as an 'establishment ploy' to exclude the Black population. At the time I couldn't understand this view, but I am beginning to see now what was meant. The 'establishment' seems to be blind to this danger; but fortunately many schools are not, and have catered for the needs of non-mainstream pupils, and will no doubt continue to do so. It would be interesting to know, in any case, which group is the 'minority' in terms of musical taste: the preferers of so-called 'mainstream music' or the others.

It is good to be able to agree with the Secretary of State for Education about something: his concurrence that there should be:

> a practical emphasis in the teaching and learning of the subject...He would therefore expect more attention to be given to the proposed Attainment Target 1: Performing and Composing than to the proposed Attainment Target 2: Listening and Appraising.

In fact, he suggests a weighting of about 2:1 in favour of practical music-making, a feature of the programme which I feel sure will be welcomed by most teachers and pupils. While in this conciliatory mood, it is worth mentioning what I think was a wise change in the title of Attainment Target 2 from 'Knowledge and Understanding' to 'Listening and Appraising'. This was to make it clearer that 'Attainment Target 2 involves not only knowledge of musical history, but knowledge of music acquired through listening to and appraising music'. The general emphasis, then, is on creativity and appreciation.

It is also intended that 'an integrated approach should be adopted for the teaching of the subject' so that 'knowledge of musical history and practical music-making' will not be isolated from each other. It is here perhaps that the emphasis on the Western cultural tradition gets most in the way. What about steel bands? What about the Indian and Japanese influences that the Beatles found stimulating? What about African percussion, Black American blues and jazz? Fortunately there is room for these in the Music curriculum — as will be seen — but its presence seems to be somewhat grudgingly included, almost as a kind of afterthought. From the point of view of the international dimension, the important paragraph is the following, taken from the General Requirements for Programmes of Study:

> Pupils should perform and listen to music in a variety of genres and styles, from different periods and cultures. The repertoire chosen should be broad and designed to extend pupils' musical experience and knowledge. It should include examples of works taken from:
>
> — the European 'classical' tradition, from its earliest roots to the present day;
>
> — folk and popular music;
>
> — music of the countries and regions of the British Isles;

— a variety of cultures, Western and non-Western.

An encouraging note follows this: 'The repertoire selected for performance should be progressively more demanding and *chosen in the light of pupils' needs, backgrounds* and stages of musical development'. (My italics.) The multicultural classroom was doubtless in mind in this recognition of different needs and backgrounds.

Having voiced a number of reservations, let us see where the specific openings for a multicultural or international dimension exist — starting with the Performing and Composing requirements (Attainment Target 1). At Key Stage 1 it is suggested that pupils 'sing traditional and modern folk songs'. There is no reason why these should not include songs from a diverse range of cultures or even in other languages, so long as they are reasonably simple. Young children are generally quick to learn by heart and enjoy (even with the correct pro-

Samuel Coleridge-Taylor
A classical composer, son of an African father from Sierra Leone and an English mother, Coleridge-Taylor's Hiawatha, African Suite, Othello *and* Faust *are just some of the noteworthy musical achievements of his short life.*

nunciation) songs or rhymes in other languages, even if they are not completely understood at the time. (I learned *The Marseillaise* from a French aunt when I was about seven, and this early unconscious exercise was a great help subsequently in acquiring a reasonable French accent.) At both Key Stage 1 and Key Stage 2 pupils are required to perform using a percussion instrument. This is a good opportunity to introduce African or South American percussion instruments if at all possible. The Nigerian 'talking drum' is excellent for 'question and answer games' as well as being interesting from the point of view of its provenance and use. Cuban bongo drums, the Chinese crash symbal, Spanish castanets — each has its special percussive qualities and evocative associations in addition. At Key Stage 3, as well as more opportunities for folk music, it is suggested that pupils 'prepare a performance of a calypso with instrumental accompaniment'. This very obviously provides an opportunity for pupils with West Indian origins or connections, but is an equally good chance to give all pupils, whether they be in multicultural communities or far from them, the challenge of creating this particular kind of composition. Another example suggested at this Key Stage is to 'improvise a solo part over a 12 bar blues sequence' — providing an excellent occasion for discussing the origins of this *genre*, and because of the social and political implications associated with it, the sombre moods which are generally characteristic. Researchers confess that documentation of the history of the blues is not always easy to acquire, but:

> What we know is that out of poverty and oppression, out of broken homes and chain gangs, out of city slums and tenant farms came the Negro blues shouter, the street singer, the itinerant guitar picker. The burden of his song was life itself — constantly changing, seeking, hoping... (Silverman, 1968)

For all too many people still today, the blues (of one kind or another) are more than entertainment; rather, they are the only way of coming to terms with the injustice and misery of their lives.

Turning now to Attainment Target 2, Listening and Appraising, at Key Stage 1 the suggestion that pupils 'discuss how music composed for different celebrations and festivals creates appropriate moods' provides obvious opportunities to consider the music relating to festivals and celebrations in different parts of the world as well as events familiar to different children from different cultural backgrounds. Rather similar in its range of possibilities is the example: 'discover what music members of their family sang and listened to when they were children and discuss any common features; (and) sing folksongs from different parts of the world and discuss their similarities and differences'. Key Stage 2 offers the occasion to 'listen to a variety of jazz bands and identify solo instruments' — again giving the chance to consider something of the origins of jazz together with the social and political implications associated. Further opportunities to consider jazz occur at Key Stage 3 when pupils might 'listen to music played by Fats Waller or Duke Ellington and use the structure of the piece as a basis for a group composition'. It is also suggested that they might listen to and assess 'two interpretations of a song by Lennon and McCartney' and 'discuss folk and popular arrangements of a familiar song', providing further openings for serious consideration of non-mainstream music.

Yehudi Menuhin and Ravi Shankar
East meets west in a bridge-building musical performance as Yehudi Menuhin learns
the art of the spntaneous composition of the raga. Yehudi Menuhin, a Unesco
Ambassador, devotes much of his energy to promoting international understanding.

An interesting suggestion relating to music and its wartime significance occurs at Key Stage 3, where pupils might be invited to 'listen to
music by Wagner and (to) discuss the use of the leitmotif; (and)
research music played and sung in wartime Britain between 1939 and
1945'. It cannot be accidental that these two ideas are placed next to
each other: Wagner's martial-style music was important to Hitler in
his mass rallies and military preparations, just as in England the
obligatory use of the national anthem, frequent singing of 'Land of
Hope and Glory' and other nationalistic songs and the many
sentimental, but at the time heartfelt, songs such as 'We'll Meet Again'
helped to sustain morale in Britain during the same period. A similar
exercise might involve the seeing of the film 'Oh, What a Lovely War!'
and discussing and analysing the music sung in the 1914–18 War. In

contrast the peace movement and Human Rights songs of the period during the major Arms Race years, the Vietnam War and the American anti-segregation movement can be studied. The messages of songs sung by Paul Robeson, Pete Seeger and Joan Baez are still relevant.

For older pupils excerpts from Benjamin Britten's *War Requiem* might in some cases be appropriate to raise issues of music in relation to war and peace. His *Noyes Fludde*, which is suitable for both older and younger pupils, deals musically with human fears and conflicts in an interesting and entertaining way. Finally, to return to the examples specifically offered in the Music programme, the suggestion at Key Stage 3 that pupils 'discuss music used for television cartoons and advertisements' can bring out the evocative capacity of music used for purposes of persuasion. I am thinking here particularly of advertisements rather than cartoons. Although music is its own language, used in relation to given situations, events and products it can acquire symbolic and persuasive power. Bach's *Orioso* can be used to appear to validate pipe-smoking; some strains of calypso music promote the sale of a tropical drink; a few suggestive bars from Beethoven's Fifth Symphony can raise morale in time of war; and so on.

Musical education is not just about entertainment and relaxation: it is about life itself. Its rhythms and melodies can support back-breaking work in the fields; raise morale and sustain energies; seduce our emotions and calm our anxieties. It is perhaps — despite its many varieties — the only truly universal language.

C. PHYSICAL EDUCATION

Sport can be an ideal means of humanising international relations and of bringing the peoples of the world together in a joint endeavour whose goal is harmonious personal development and the upholding of the ethical values of society in the spirit of the Olympic ideal.
(from the Declaration of the Intergovernmental Committee for Physical Education and Sport, UNESCO, 1988)

We recommend that the place, role and prestige of physical and sports education in school and in society should be enhanced by giving it a significant and obligatory share of the curriculum, by ensuring that it is taught by qualified personnel and that it is allocated the necessary facilities and installations.
(from the Declaration of the 2nd International Conference of Ministers and Senior Officials for PE & Sport, UNESCO, 1988)

The dread of beatings! Dread of being late;
And, the greatest dread of all, the dread of games.
(John Betjeman, 'Summoned by Bells')

That physical health is 'a good thing' few people would doubt, and that physical education can contribute to this is more or less axiomatic. A well-worn Roman saying reminds us that a 'healthy mind' needs its 'healthy body' to carry it about! How far then does the National Curriculum contribute to individual physical well-being, and to social and international health, in turn?

Although covering a wide range of activities, the Physical Education schedule has the merit of simplicity, being 'based on a single attainment target encompassing planning, performing and evaluating, with the main emphasis on active performing'. In preparation for physical exertion pupils are encouraged to understand their bodies (their capabilities and limitations); in practice high standards of bodily and mental control are expected; and afterwards self-evaluation of their performance is required. All of this is unexceptionable: planning-capability, self-discipline and self-knowledge are all socially desirable attributes. The physical fitness which is the desired end of the activities should promote a sense of well-being and confidence, both of which are conducive to good citizenship. And among the general requirements to be taught through all areas of activity and at all key stages are several other socially desirable qualities. Notably, pupils should be taught:

— to observe the rules of personal hygiene;

— to be aware of the effects and consequences of their actions on others and on the environment;

— to observe the conventions of fair play, honest competition and good sporting behaviour;

— to cope with both success and failure...

In addition, for a number of activities they should 'develop an awareness of basic safety practices such as the Green Cross Code'.

The six areas of activity in the Physical Education programme are: athletic activities, dance, games, gymnastic activities, outdoor and adventurous activities and swimming. At key stage 1 pupils should experience at least five of these; at key stage 2 they should normally experience six; at key stage 3 they should experience a minimum of four; and at key stage 4 they should study at least two.

Athletics and gymnastics are two areas of activity which provide opportunities for a pupil to promote and measure his or her own progress. Competition with others is of course possible; but competition with *oneself*, beating one's previous record or achievement and so gaining in confidence and stature, are equally possible. *Swimming* is obviously valuable for similar reasons of general progress and fitness, with the added importance of the safety factor — that it might prove life-saving in some future circumstance. In all of these there is of course an aesthetic factor, but this factor becomes pre-eminent in *dance* where expressive movements relating to different moods and music are added to the poise and grace necessary for all physical achievement. At Key Stage 4 pupils undertaking dance should 'be given opportunities to describe, interpret and evaluate all aspects of dance including choreography, performance, cultural and historical contexts and production'. This clearly provides an opening for developing inter-cultural understanding of dance styles, customs and motivations from different peoples are sympathetically studied; and more particularly if meetings and demonstrations can be arranged representative of some of these traditions. *Outdoor and Adventurous Activities* offer some of the best opportunities for developing qualities of independence, team work, sharing and leadership; and leadership of a kind where, it is suggested, they 'learn to appreciate the contributions made by individual members of a team of group'. 'Working in small groups', 'recording and evaluating', 'developing skills necessary for the activity' are required; and they should also learn 'to assess and respond to challenges in a variety of contexts and conditions'. I cannot think of a much better way of preparing for an unknown future in an unpredictable, yet interconnected, world. That leaves us with one further area, *Games* — which for a variety of reasons deserves separate consideration.

From age 8 to age 14 *games* are a compulsory element of the National Curriculum. Many school-children will welcome this, but not all. John Betjeman is not the only schoolboy to have experienced an inordinate fear of games. Philip Stubbs in *The Anatomie of Abuses* (1583) wrote: 'As concerning football, I protest unto you that it may rather be called a friendly kind of fight than a play or recreation — a bloody and murthering practise than a fellowly sport or pastime'. Maybe for similar reasons the Duke of Wellington is said to have suggested that 'The battle of Waterloo was won on the playing fields of Eton'! Maurice Baring, in *The Puppet show of Memory* (1922) made an important observation: 'There is a vast difference between games and play. Play is played for fun, but games are deadly serious and you do not play them to enjoy yourself'. One must ask why games, rather than say 'outdoor and adventurous activities' or 'dance' was made the one compulsory element at Key Stage 3. Certainly, games provide many occasions for co-operation: passing to a team-mate (by kicking, throwing or hitting a ball, according to the game); by moving in a co-ordinated fashion; by being ready to receive a pass, and so on. But co-operation in all the other physical activities of the curriculum is also possible.

I am worried when I think of the Duke of Wellington and of Betjeman! Of all the areas of the PE curriculum, 'games' is the only one that necessarily involves the language of war, and I quote: 'attacking', 'defending','invasion', 'opponents'. Moreover, while at all Key Stages pupils should 'respond readily to instructions and signals within established routines, and follow the relevant rules and codes' — it applies in 'games' perhaps, most of all. The wording of this is vastly better than 'must learn to obey authority without question' (which was the issue at the Nurenberg Trials). However, there is a worrying phrase, 'refrain from showing dissent' that comes in at Key Stage 4, presumably in connection with games. I can understand the import of this phrase: football and even cricket and tennis are brought into disrepute by ugly scenes of wrangling, even occasionally violence, between players and those appointed to ensure fair play (referees, umpires, etc). But I shouldn't like to see the requirement 'refrain from showing dissent' generalised into too many aspects of life in a democratic society. Perhaps this is quibbling, but having seen PE taught by ex-army physical instructors with more firmly-fixed ideas about discipline than about democracy, I think the point is worth making. In the end, of course, everything depends upon *how* the subject is taught, whether the emphasis is on co-operation rather than competition, whether explanations for rules are given, whether the weakest members are given support, and so on.

Fortunately, particular games are not stipulated in the National Curriculum, and so there is a wide range available (depending, of course, upon the availability of resources) from rugby football to, presumably, table-tennis. Pupils are to 'be made aware of the historical, social and cultural issues associated with the activities undertaken'. From the international point of view, football provides historical and current links with Europe in particular; cricket with countries of the Commonwealth; badminton with Far Eastern countries — Malaysia, China, etc. Opportunities for international sporting events may be infrequent for school games, but pupils can be made aware of future possibilities. The curriculum, incidentally, includes the important advice that pupils should 'learn appropriate behaviour when spectating and when travelling to and from events'. Whether such advice will necessarily be heeded in the mass excitement and hysteria of the sporting events they subsequently attend is another matter; but it's a good thing to learn it.

UNESCO and the Olympic Committee put high value on the importance of international sport. At the Second International Conference of Ministers and Senior Officials Responsible for Physical Education and Sport in 1988, the President of the International Olympic Committee said:

> Independence and collaboration in a spirit of mutual respect —
> these are the watchwords we defend with deep conviction...
> Today, more strongly than ever before, our primary responsibility
> is to serve as a bridge, a link between viewpoints, sometimes
> conflicting, always different. By uniting beneath the flag with the
> five interlinked rings the most different peoples, the most total
> opposites that humanity has produced, and providing them with
> a unique and precious opportunity to mingle, talk to each other,
> perhaps get to know each other, appreciate and understand one
> another, the Olympic Movememnt is helping to fulfil the noblest
> mission mankind can perform — to allow friendship, brother-
> hood, understanding and peace to reign.

The 'Declaration' produced by members of the same Conference speaks of:

Ensuring the widespread practice of physical and recreational activities is one of the most effective and least costly ways of improving the health, hygiene and well-being of a population. Sport (it adds) is also an invaluable instrument to fight against the social evils such as alcoholism and the use of drugs...

Among other things the Declaration draws attention to the importance of physical education 'to the disadvantaged sectors of the population' applying both to the world spectrum and to disadvantaged sectors within better-off states.

These lofty ideals regarding international sport are not universally shared. E.M. Forster, in *Two Cheers for Democracy* (1957), offers a different perspective:

It is international sport that helps to kick the world downhill. Started by foolish athletes, who thought it would promote understanding, it is supported today by the desire for political prestige and by interests involved in gate monies. It is completely harmful.

Harsh words, but not without an element of truth that has to be heeded; The Conference already referred to was aware of these dangers, and the *Final Report of the Intergovernmental Committee for Sport* (1988) with which the Conference was linked made a strong comment in its 'Declaration':

We cannot remain unconcerned when athletes take drugs that distort the physical abilities of the human organism, which could drive people away from sport. We cannot remain silent at the unbridled search for profit in sport, at violence, at exaggerated national sentiments among players and spectators, at the pressures exerted by sponsors, or at the emergence of athletes who seek to win at any price, even at the expense of their health... at especially excessive commercialization and professional practices... It is not a question of not producing champions but of ensuring that they win fairly and are genuine examples for the young people of the world to follow.

One of the problems facing international sport today is the availability of athletic records. For the ancient Greeks, every event was a new beginning: the absence of accurate timing of former speeds, heights and lengths meant that there was no burden of beating former records of achievement. There is something unhealthy about forcing the human body over implacable figures simply because someone, somewhere in the world reached that figure before. All of these problems

militate to a greater or lesser extent against the absolute value of international sport; but on balance it is probably true that the gains are
greater than the losses. It is perhaps up to teachers of PE to try, at least,
to create the attitudes to ensure that this is so.

There remain a number of additional issues in a multicultural society
that have to be borne in mind by teachers. Among these is the assumption of a genetic relationship between race and physical skills. There is
no doubt that a number of Black sportsmen and women have done
extremely well in running and in games. But a tendency to regard this
as having a racial connection is misfounded and politically and
socially dangerous. It can become linked to the 'noble savage' image,
contrasting physical with intellectual inheritance; and it can provide a
smokescreen to obscure what is probably a major reason for some of
the successes that have been achieved: the need for excluded or
marginalized Blacks to find success routes when inappropriate or
inadequate educational provision has left them disadvantaged in
other areas. Sport in these circumstances provides a high level of motivation. More sinister still, perhaps, is the process described by
Carrington in 'Sport as a Side-track' (1982), whereby academically
able black pupils are sometimes nudged into sporting achievement at
the expense of the more intellectually-geared careers they might
otherwise have followed. This phenomenon is the sadder because the
sidetracking is often intended, in good faith, to benefit the pupils
concerned.

Another of the issues needing careful and tactful handling in a multicultural community is the need to ensure that pupils are not made to
feel out of things for religious reasons. Muslim girls, for example, may
have to be given special consideration so that they can be involved
with their fellows without flouting traditional expectations in regard
to dress or activities.

Before leaving the Physical Education curriculum, one final observation is worth making — in relation to the importance of sport as a
lifelong leisure activity. At the UNESCO Conference of Ministers
already mentioned, Mr Marat Gramov raised this matter forcefully:

> Physical culture and sport are a powerful focus of leisure-time
> activity. Let me give you this example — in sixteen days, almost
> three thousand million people watched the 1988 Olympic Games
> on television....Hundreds of millions of people spend their free
> time at sports events. No other form of leisure-time activity
> attracts such a vast following as sport....Sport and physical

culture, because of their humanistic essence, with the ability to bring peoples closer together and contribute to the development of contacts, co-operation and mutual understanding between countries, are playing an increasingly significant role in the life of the whole international community.

Like music, art and literature, sport can have a special value at times of unemployment, perhaps, in providing positive activity, interest and motivation to people otherwise without a sense of purpose. The National Curriculum, whether or not its designers had this in mind, encourages students at Key Stage 4 to 'make use of the facilities at local clubs and leisure centres' and to 'use the local resources for water-based activities'. It is hoped that the funding will be available for them to be able to continue to use such valuable facilities when they leave school.

Chapter 7

Religious Education and Citizenship in a Plural Society

Everyone has the right to freedom of thought, conscience and religion; this right includes freedom to change his religion or belief, and freedom, either alone or in community with others and in public or private, to manifest his religion or belief in teaching, practice, worship and observance. (Universal Declaration of Human Rights, Article 18)

The one Religion is beyond all reach. Imperfect men put it into such language as they can command, and their words are interpreted by other men equally imperfect...Everybody is right from his own standpoint, but it is not impossible that everybody is wrong. Hence the necessity for tolerance, which does not mean indifference to one's own faith, but a more intelligent and purer love for it.
(M.K.Gandhi)

We are not saying that schools do not teach citizenship, but we would like to see greater rigour in the curriculum and its planning... The suggestions in the report are not designed to give pupils a ready-made kit of values but to help them assemble their own.
(Duncan Graham, Chairman, National Curriculum Council)

Note: The author wishes to acknowledge the co-operation of Dr Jagdish Gundara for material incorporated this chapter.

This chapter is addressed to two important areas of the National Curriculum — Citizenship and Religious Education — and to a third area, Human Rights, to the promotion of which the state is formally committed. Although neither Citizenship nor Religious Education are among the core or foundation subjects, they are explicitly included in the 1988 Education Act as essential elements of the National Curriculum. Citizenship Education is to be distributed among the other subjects as a cross-dimensional theme, and provisions for RE are to be set out by local Standing Advisory Councils (SACRE) in accordance with the principles laid down; and a daily act of worship is prescribed for all state schools, except for certain specifically negotiated exceptions. These three elements — citizenship, religious education and human rights — are considered together here because of their close interconnection.

A. RELIGIOUS EDUCATION

UK citizens are varied in their religious affiliation or quite frequently have no affiliation at all; and so the 1988 Education Act has had to take account of the rights of individuals. Whether it has taken sufficient account of the situation is one of the questions which has to be considered, and a case will be made out for a secular solution when, as is inevitable in due course, the Act is revised. But, pending the changes which a review might bring about, we also address the possibilities within the Act as it currently stands. Fortunately, the Education Act has not completely ignored the advice given in the working paper by HM Inspectorate Curriculum 11-16 (1977):

> ...there is a widespread recognition that children who are growing up in a multi-racial society need to know something of those major world faiths now found in the community which represent the deeply held convictions of fellow citizens. Religious education in county schools is most appropriately seen as an introduction to man's religious quest and some of its contemporary expressions in belief and practice, rather than a process of induction into a particular religious tradition.

It is noteworthy that the working paper here refers to children in society at large not just to those in specific local conditions with minority concerns; also that it speaks of 'man's religious *quest*' and rejects the idea of 'induction' into a particular tradition. The reference to 'major world faiths' is a reminder that a multi-racial, or multi-faith society has at its disposal the ready means to share insights valuable for international understanding. The paper is wisely careful about the need for students to understand the nature of religious language — that it is not empirical, but largely 'evocative and imaginative', using 'symbolism, the language of myth and parable, metaphor and analogy, to point to those areas of personal and community experience which are at the limits of understanding'. The allusiveness of religious language on the one hand and the varied convictions, levels of interest and emotional and spiritual capacities of the pupils on the other hand demand sensitivity and flexibility on the part of the teacher. The relevant section of the working paper concludes:

> Religious education may provide a basis for understanding the search for meaning in life and an invitation to share in that, but it is the pupil's own life which will provide the experiences that shape his response and test its consistency and quality.

Interestingly, in its reference specifically to Christianity, the Inspectorate's working paper paved the way (perhaps inadvertently) for the formulation of the 1988 Act we have now when it stated:

> Since for most children in county schools it is the most familiar form in which they encounter expression of religion and since it has had a formative influence upon this country's culture it is generally accepted that Christianity should retain a central place in the subject.

The Act, as now passed, requires a non-denominational daily act of worship for all pupils (though not necessarily in the form of a 'whole school' assembly) which must be 'wholly or mainly of a broadly Christian character'. The terms 'mainly' and 'broadly' fortunately allow a certain room for manoeuvre. According to the Act 'collective worship is of a broadly Christian character if it reflects the broad traditions of Christian belief without being distinctive of any particular denomination' (Part 1, 7(2)). Here again 'reflects' allows a certain latitude in the interpretation of the Act. Moreover, schools can take into account 'any circumstances relating to the family backgrounds of the pupils concerned which are relevant for determining the character of collective worship which is appropriate in their case; and their ages and aptitudes'. In particularly problematic cases heads (having obtained the approval of governors and parents) can apply to the local Standing Advisory Council for a 'determination' that the requirements of the Christian collective worship should not apply for their school or for a particular category of pupils. As with the 1944 Act parents still have the right to withdraw their children, and staff have the right to withdraw themselves from any or all the acts of worship.

On the face of it, all this seems very fair: the law allows a degree of freedom to individuals and groups in the community. But whether the current solution allows '*equality* before the law' is open to question. In their anxiety to avoid what some of the more extreme policy-makers called a 'mish-mash multifaith approach' the legislators have created a two-valued situation giving dominance and prestige to Christianity and marginalizing other faiths. Withdrawal is possible and separate religious education and worship are allowed, but the alternatives to Christianity are inevitably devalued. The ideal of sharing for the sake of mutual enlightenment is still possible, but is made more difficult than it needs to be.

One small development to be welcomed is the change from the term 'Religious Instruction' in the 1944 Act to 'Religious Education' in the new act. The implications of this point to a more objective approach to religion(s) rather than an induction into a specific faith. This could be seen as a small step towards a more secular and open approach. But what are the arguments in favour of a totally secular education?

Let us consider first some situations where education is closely bound up with state-dominant religion or subject to a theocracy. In Northern Ireland the tradition of denominational separatism in education (although only one of the factors in the present situation) has con-tributed over the years to a climate of fear and distrust. In Iran and Pakistan the educational dominance of Islam has created difficulties — often tragedies — for followers of other faiths. In India, perhaps as a reaction to Islamic fundamentalism and to Sikh militancy, attempts by militant Hindus to create a state monopoly of Hinduism have already had some tragic results. Israel's state Judaism has not helped solve the Palestinian problem. And in our own history the persecution of Jews, Catholics and Protestants by turns has been associated with the dominant state religion or denomination.

By contrast, France, the USA and countries of the former Communist block have, in their different ways, opted for secularism. In France Catholicism has remained reasonably healthy, while Protestants' and non-believers' views and life-styles are respected; and Muslim pupils are not obliged to withdraw from any school activities or opt for separate education on account of their faith. In America, secular state education has done nothing to reduce religious commitment or church attendance. On the contrary, television evangelism and religious fundamentalism are 'big business' with three Christian broadcasting

Opposite: 'Quot homines, tot sententiae' *(So many men, so many minds, Terence, 160BC) or* Why can't they get their act together?

networks and 40 TV stations with a full-time diet of religious pro-grammes. The specific virtue of this efflorescence is not part of the present argument! Nor is the fact that large numbers of schools are being set up in the USA to teach fundamentalist religion — partly in opposition to the evolution-based science teaching which is normal in American state schools as in British schools (and is of course authorised in the science programme of the National Curriculum). At least American state schools cannot be held *responsible* for the aberrations of extremist groups.

It is becoming more and more clear that the ultra-secularist approach of Communist education was far from successful in eliminating religious belief in the former eastern block. The Freedom of Conscience law approved by the Soviet legislature in September 1990 was welcomed by millions of Soviet believers now given the right to study religion in their homes and in private schools. In the first of such schools icons quickly replaced portraits of Marx and Lenin and prayers are offered before and after lessons, according to a *Guardian* report (27/11/90). In Poland, way back in 1984, the state finally had to compromise with the innumerable schools that insisted on displaying crucifixes despite the legal ban on them. Changes in Poland have accelerated since then. Witness an interesting observation from a Polish workshop on education reported in *The Friend* (28/6/91):

> One special issue was the introduction of religious education in schools, often taught by priests. Parents can withdraw their children, but there are strong social pressures not to do so. Many teachers already see an adverse effect. While the church was in opposition to the communist state, children were keen to go to the church for religious instruction, but now it is just a school subject and many dislike it.

It appears in general then that secular education does not make people less religious than they would otherwise be. On the contrary. And compulsory religious education in schools fails to make people more religious. Moreover, in some cases it can be counter-productive in terms of the quality of citizenship emerging. Tolerance and mutual understanding, necessary in any society, are particularly important in multi-faith and multi-ethnic communities. Fortunately there are examples on record of successful efforts to bring together pupils of different faiths in a secular situation of equality. Jews and Arabs are educated together in the Neve Shalom interfaith community, for example, on the borders of Israel. A spokesman in an *Independent* article (4/3/89) explained, 'We don't ask people to give up anything of their identity, religion or culture'. The school is not a 'melting pot', nor is it satisfied with mere 'coexistence'; through conflict management it aims 'to achieve equality and *co-operation*'. Similarly in South Africa on the initiative of the New Era School Trust (v. *Guardian* (17/10/89) multi-racial schools are being set up where the pupils are being taught in an atmosphere of equality 'to understand and tolerate the diversity in traditions, values and religious beliefs among their companions'.

As Europe becomes more and more integrated, modern European nations, like other nation states, need to face the issue of secularism. Societal diversities may necessitate regulation, and it is best that this is based on consensus amongst the constituent groups and communities within Europe. To promote tolerance as a fact rather than simply a social ideal we need to have clear definitions about the secular nature of European societies and the rights and obligations of various citizens and groups. Religious *instruction* clearly belongs to the private domain (where apparently it flourishes best anyway) and not to the public sector. Religious *knowledge* (or religious *education*, the term adopted in the 1988 Act), on the other hand, rightly has a place in the public domain where the comparative study of religions and deeper spiritual understanding can be encouraged through the education systems.

A low-key, secular approach to religious education, strengthening the legitimacy of all citizens and reducing fears of assimilation through social pressure can help to reduce the danger of mushrooming fundamentalisms proclaiming 'the *only* solution' to the world's spiritual and political problems and disparaging all alternatives. The current rise of fundamentalism among some faith communities is very largely the result of the 'siege mentality' which is the natural reaction of self-defence to unbearable pressures by groups which have been marginalized or made the scapegoats of social problems. Since the symbol systems of religion tend to strike a stronger chord than the diffuse systems of secular life, it is understandable that anxious or undervalued individuals will seek social cohesion and legitimacy in the security of would-be fundamental 'certainties'. The rise of such commanding belief systems in modern states is perhaps a reflection of how governments have failed so far to provide a safe and secure framework for diverse faith communities. It is also partly attributable to empty assertions of human rights which are not accompanied by effective measures to ensure their implementation.

Obviously, conflicts will inevitably occur from time to time between the state and various belief systems, or between one belief system and another. Currently these are resolved by *ad hoc* pragmatic solutions. It may be that a clearly defined bill of rights with constitutional solutions to the issues needs to be explored. Within such a legal frame-work, fundamental human rights of all citizens ought to be guaranteed. The European Convention on Human Rights and the various international covenants represent the beginnings of a solution to the challenges of a plural society — but they are not a substitute for binding national legal codes. However, this is an issue for human rights groups and lawyers and is outside the scope of our present discussion which must return to the Religious Education requirements of the 1988 Act as they now stand.

It is reasonable that Christianity should have a significant place in religious education in the United Kingdom — it permeates so much of British culture and history; our holidays (holy days), for example, are largely based on the Christian calendar, and curiosity alone would want some explanation of their origin, as of many other aspects of our social organisation. What is disappointing is the pressure put upon non-Christians to join in a daily act of worship or lessons where they might feel ill at ease or to be marginalized by removal. A spokesman for the Islamic Society for the Promotion of Religious Tolerance expressed the point succinctly (*Guardian*,28/6/88):

> ...non-Christians will have to leave the class and their classmates... and that will emphasise their feelings of being 'different'. Those who remain in the class will be seen as privileged by virtue of being Christian, and those who are out will learn from an early age that to identify as British one must be Christian. We believe this is a recipe for intolerance...The only universal thing it will bring is resentment.

Similarly a *Guardian* article (22/1/91) pointed out that:

> Some Hindu parents, supportive of an open religious education which explores Christianity and the other faiths represented in Britain are deeply offended at the potential divisiveness of the worship clause.

However, those of us concerned with improving the multicultural situation, and the international understanding that can be developed from this are obliged to make the best of the situation as it is. The same *Guardian* article points out how some schools ease the situation by their interpretation of the word 'collective' in the expression 'a *collective* act of worship':

> They do not provide a corporate act of worship in which everybody is assumed to be worshipping together with common assumptions and beliefs. Rather, they provide an educational experience for the whole of the school in which individuals have the opportunity to worship.

They stress the 'shared moral and spiritual values' as in many of the creative junior school 'assemblies' of the past. Thus they avoid 'fragmentation of the school' and 'emphasise the importance of learning from one another, acknowledging one another's special days and sharing and reflecting on common human experiences'.

Again, the expression 'broad traditions of Christian belief' facilitates a wide spectrum of interpretation from rigid orthodoxy to, for example, the Quaker emphasis on openness, 'responding to that of God in every person', seeking spiritual enlightenment from those of other faiths and (where appropriate) of none, and recognising the value of silent worship — something which other denominations are nowadays frequently incorporating in their services. It is not difficult to find the writings of many 'open' Christians whose commitment and depth of study has lead them beyond the confines of narrow dogmatism to ideas and insights that have universal reference. Albert Schweitzer, the Franco-German whose generous missionary work was regrettably tainted with the paternalism of his age, was nevertheless a great spirit, and his theological and philosophical ideas drawing on a study of all the major world religions achieve their climax in his universal principal of 'reverence for life'. The Russian Christian Leo Tolstoy provides material which overrides narrow boundaries. In a letter to an enquirer, J. Shikunev, for example, he wrote:

> You must also know that Christ was not the only wise man. In various centuries, from various races, we have had many other enlightened teachers — Buddha and Krishna in India, Confucius and Lao-Tze in China, while the ancient Persians had their Zoroaster, and the Arabs Mohammed. In every instance the doctrine of these wise and exalted teachers has met with the same fate as Christianity. The most important parts have been corrupted and killed... For one thing only must we take thought — how to lead our lives in accordance with the will of God and the dictates of our conscience. Neither ceremonies nor miracles will

Martin Luther King, Jr (1929-1968)

A man who combined active Christianity with Gandhian 'satyagraha', Martin Luther King went to jail more than thirty times during his crusade against injustice. His name has become 'a symbol of courage and hope for oppressed people everywhere'.

ever teach us this; we can only learn it from the actual lives of wise men. Such is the real teaching of Christ, as I understand it...

The famous speech of the American Christian, Martin Luther King, — 'I have a dream...' is too well-known to need quotation here; nor do we need reminding that his life and work have a significance well above narrow sectarian interests. The anti-apartheid South African Archbishop Desmond Tutu, the anti-Nazi German theologian Deitrich Bonhoeffer provide examples of universalistic Christian responses to oppression. E.F.Schumacher writes from a Christian perspective modified by Buddhist ideas. Then there are the generous references to and reflections of Christianity in the life and teaching of M.K.Gandhi:

I have endeavoured to study the Bible (he writes). I consider it as part of my scriptures. The spirit of the Sermon on the Mount competes almost on equal terms with the Bhagavad Gita for the domination of my heart. I yield to no Christian in the strength of devotion with which I sing 'Lead kindly light' and several other inspired hymns of a similar nature... (v. Duncan, 1983)

Writing in his *Autobiography* of his friendship in Durban with the Christian, Mr Spencer Walton, Gandhi says:

I do not recollect his ever having invited me to embrace Christianity. But he placed his life as an open book before me... We knew the fundamental differences between us. Any amount of discussion could not efface them. Yet even differences prove helpful where there are tolerance, charity and truth.

Finally, it is possible to find expressions of Christian ideals from outside the confines of Christianity itself. Dr Kenneth Kaunda, for example, until recently President of Zambia, writing in a section called 'The Humanist's view of the future' (in *Letter to my Children*, 1973), says:

> Whether or not you have been convinced by your upbringing and the teachings of the Church that there is a God above who created us, it is always better to stand for truth against error, love rather hate, service in preference to selfishness, sacrifice in place of self-preservation. For these are the qualities which finally change the world for the better, and it is a deeply satisfying thing to know that you have left the world, your society and generation a little better than you found them.

And again:

> If countries want peace they must understand that the problem in essence is not one of treaties, world organisations or codes of humanitarian law. Peace must first of all be established by transforming Man from within. The source of all evil, all wars, all injustice, lies within us. It is not 'out there'...The real enemy has occupied not the top of our minds in vain imaginings but the bottom of our hearts in devilish pride.

Thus, on the one hand, material of 'a broadly Christian character' can be imported from non-Christian sources; and, on the other hand, the breadth of a good deal of material from within Christian sources extends well beyond narrow and confined orthodoxies to encompass universal ideals.

In fact, the closer one goes to the heart of Christianity (as perhaps of any religion) the less one is bound by dogmatic exclusiveness and the more universalistic is the essence. There is probably enough globally relevant potential to provide material for several school years in the Beatitudes and the two verses from the Gospel of St Matthew:

> For I was an hungred, and ye gave me meat: I was thirsty, and ye gave me drink: I was a stranger, and ye took me in: Naked, and ye clothed me: I was sick, and ye visited me: I was in prison, and ye came unto me.

Lessons or assemblies arising from such a source could lead into the work of Oxfam, the Save the Children Fund, Amnesty International, Unesco, the Howard League for Prison Reform and similar organisations as well as raising such issues as relief for famines and disasters,

Human Rights and other global matters. Furthermore, such considerations would be more than 'broadly Christian', they would be 'essentially Christian' as well as sharing in essence with the bases of other faiths. Learning about these other faiths, as about Christianity, is another equally important matter: but in each case (including Christianity) their history, doctrines, sacraments, etc, need to be studied objectively and tolerantly. There is no room for proselytising or indoctrination in state schools.

These observations are not offered as counsels of perfection, but as suggestions as to how to begin to make the best of an imperfect situation. The present author, a Christian, remembers a deeply spiritual experience in a public secondary school in a poor neighbourhood in Bombay where children offered prayers in turn from their different faiths — Buddhist, Hindu, Christian, Muslim and Jain. The assembly of several hundred boys and girls facing a centre-piece of beautifully arranged flowers, was conducted with the utmost reverence and simplicity. This is presumably the kind of event that is termed a 'mish-mash multi-faith approach'. I think Jesus would have felt much more at home there than some politicians! We need to ask ourselves what kind of religious education and religious experiences are the best preparation for citizenship in a multi-faith society. Maybe there is room for a little 'mish-mash' — a number of New Testament passages, stories and parables affirm that such an approach is, at the very least, 'broadly Christian'.

It is the responsibility of the Standing Advisory Councils for Religious Education (SACREs) to provide specific recommendations and advice for teachers to help them implement this area of the National Curriculum. In a recent Analysis of SACRE Reports (NCC,1992) concern is expressed that a number of schools are not yet meeting the statutory requirements to teach RE to all pupils and that the time allocated to the teaching of RE has generally decreased since 1988. There is also anxiety about the shortage of primary school teachers with any formal qualifications in RE. Perhaps there is a link between these problems and the unrealistic nature of the National Curriculum requirements for Religious Education in a multicultural society? Since the report also states that the number of pupils withdrawn from RE continues to be very small there is a strong argument for ensuring that those participating in the lessons and acts of worship are not made to feel alienated. It is to be hoped that the advice eventually offered by the SACREs will give the expression 'broadly Christian' its widest possible interpretation.

B. CITIZENSHIP

The common denominator between Religious Education and Citizenship is essentially *values* education. What shared values help people to live harmoniously together in a given community or state? The National Curriculum Council suggests that the 'values of a civilised society' include 'justice, democracy and respect for the rule of law'. Teachers should therefore promote these values and 'teach pupils to be honest and truthful'. Pupils, according to the NCC *Report* should learn that 'all citizens can and must be equal' and that 'Britain is a multicultural, multi-ethnic, multifaith and multilingual society'. They should understand the nature of the family and their own place in the community. Good citizenship, according to the report, also involves an appreciation of the importance of wealth creation, and an understanding of the role of the police and of the trade unions in society. The Council recommends, however, that the specific study of politics should not begin until the age of 14. Citizenship is expected to feature in all subjects, and the NCC would like to see greater rigour in this aspect of curriculum planning. The report 'is intended as a framework for curriculum debate...not a blueprint or a set of lesson plans'. According to the NCC Chairman, Duncan Graham: 'the suggestions in the report are not designed to give pupils a ready-made kit of values but to help them assemble their own'.

The values promoted here are unexceptionable — truthfulness, honesty, justice, equality, mutual respect, etc. — and a reasonable degree of emphasis on citizens' *responsibilities* and obligations is appropriate; but perhaps there is room also for a critical recognition of citizens' *rights* in a democracy. Also, it is rather extraordinary in today's contracted world that there is no mention of the need to be aware of supra-national organisations such as the United Nations and its agencies, or the International Red Cross or Amnesty International,for example. True the term 'citizen' is related to 'city', but it is inappropriate in twentieth century education to use it in a parochial medieval sense. Teachers have a responsibility to enlarge the concept in recognition that we are all global citizens now — and our economic, political and cultural organisation is inextricably inter-connected. The recognition that Britain is a pluralist society provides an opportunity to explore some of the implications inherent in the idea that in some respects Britain is a microcosm of the wider world, and it is to be hoped that teachers will take advantage of this in looking at relevant international issues.

At each stage of pupils' development the NCC report on education for citizenship recommends considering two aspects of citizenship: (1) the idea of *community*, and (2) *democracy in action*. This is probably a helpful division. Teachers concerned with conflict-management and peace education have always stressed the importance of learning from the pupils' own experience of community in the first place, and developing a degree of political understanding from this. Looking at *community* education the Report suggests that in the first stage (6-7 years) pupils should be encouraged to co-operate, discuss in their groups, help their partners, take turns and explore responses to bullying. At 8-11 years they can begin to investigate links with Europe, survey the languages spoken by class members, learn about the nature of citizenship from a study of early civilisations and investigate anti-social behaviour. The consequences of individual actions (such as vandalism) to others are to be considered at age 12-14, as well as some of the challenges of a pluralist society — e.g. family life, employment prospects and the role of the media. At 14-16 years the study of a recent census is recommended, also active community service with the handicapped or elderly, and some study of child benefit, problems of leaving home, etc. *Democracy in action* begins at the first stage (6-7 years) with decisions about what jobs need to be done in class, creating a rota, distinguishing between employment and leisure (including perhaps a visit to a swimming pool to learn how it is run). Public services can be studied at the next stage (8-11) comparing those of 100 years ago with those of today. At 12-14 years examples of local planning can be studied from newspapers, and employment and leisure examined together with health and safety considerations. Finally at 14-16 the study of a local election is recommended, including the interviewing of voters and party officials and the debating of candidates' views. Some consideration of public services and the welfare state is also suggested at this stage.

Given such a programme as a basis, it is quite possible (and desirable) to extend references and make comparisons with situations in other parts of the world, and bring out interconnections where appropriate. There remains, however, a problem which has to be faced in our society as at present constituted. And that is, how does one ensure that all the pupils have a true sense of being 'citizens' in British society? To what extent do different pupils identify with the country they are living in and feel the sense of nationhood which must be the basis of active citizenship?

In England, as in the rest of what is worryingly becoming 'fortress Europe', there are problems about the status of settlers, particularly in relation to their 'belongingness'. Different formulations and terminologies are used to exclude them from the body politic. Hence, how long does a 'migrant' or an 'immigrant' remain an immigrant? Do the children of immigrants born in Europe see themselves as living in 'host' countries? How do 'ethnic minorities' differ in their self-identification from 'historic or traditional minorities'; and how, for example, does a Scottish-born Sikh regard himself in terms of nation-hood and citizenship? European states have long been a hotch-potch (or 'mish-mash'!) of different languages, regions, social classes, families, religions and traditions. The ethnicity (in terms of racial difference) which was an issue for Normans and Anglo-Saxons has long ago dissolved, as have many subsequent ethnic tensions; but the mythology suggests that European societies have only recently become diversified, and that the onus of diversity in European societies lies on the immigrants. European nation states are presented as being inherently monolithic, monocultural and monolingual, which leads to the common perception that the groups who are seen as being different are also the cause of the problems created by social diversity in Europe.

Self-image is partly a product of how others see us. Thus Europeans are encouraged by what they read and hear about their 'civilization' and their 'higher culture' to believe that they must be civilised and highly cultured, comfortably ignoring any evidence to the contrary. The Belgian Minister for the Interior said in a speech in October 1987:

> We risk being like the Roman people, being invaded by Barbarians, who are the Arabs, Moroccans, Yugoslavs and Turks. People who have come from far away and have nothing in common with our civilization.

Nearer home, the reaction to the adoption of a black parliamentary candidate for Cheltenham's conservative party brought the reaction: 'Why the hell choose a nigger?' from the Minister for Tourism, and from another party member the objection that one shouldn't 'kow-tow to the coloureds'. This kind of thing does little to enhance respect for the black community among whites and angers and alienates Blacks, inevitably (one would imagine) discouraging some from involvement in 'active citizenship'.

Constructions of European nationhood are consciously (or uncon-sciously) created, recreated, manipulated and mystified to enhance or ensure the continuity of established nationalisms with the result that some children grow up with the comforting notion that they belong to a kind of exclusive civilised club, while children of other groups may be excluded, dominated, marginalized or distanced by being referred to as 'barbarians', 'ethnics', 'migrants' or 'orientals'. They are always, made to feel, 'the other'; and in many cases they experience not only poverty, but denial of legal entitlements, and negation of political and human rights. Democratic involvement and citizenship must be predicated on equality and equal access to power. Should our degree of 'active citizenship' depend upon the status of our passport, or the number of times we have been stopped by the police or refused a job or flat because of our ethnicity? It is not surprising that xenophobia and racism towards the immigrant population by scapegoating them for all that is wrong with our society often leads to a 'siege mentality' amongst immigrant and other minorities to defend themselves and their interests. Rastafarianism is perhaps an expression of this inevitable reaction. The black communities in Brixton, Southall and Harmondsworth arise from more complex reasons than this, but self-defence and self-help are contributory. The territorial basis of the Scots and the Welsh has constitutional recognition; but these new settlements are more politically precarious. And it it would be surprising if some of this sense of instability were not reflected in attitudes to citizenship.

However, the very fact that John Taylor, the black candidate for Cheltenham was selected despite grumblings from the old guard is cause for hope. The way for change is open, and the role of educators is to assist in the deconstruction of the 'dominant-self' image wherever it might exist, and however it is defined. The process entails enabling the 'other' to speak for themselves and to articulate their cultures, histories and hopes. Ways of perceiving ourselves and others have got to be revised if citizenship is to have any meaning and future. In 1977 HM Inspectorate's working paper *Curriculum 11-16* included a valuable section on Political Competence. There is no reason why much of the wisdom included in this publication should not be incorporated in schemes for Citizenship Education, either before or after the age of 14, as seems most appropriate. The report reminds us that 'political competence in a democracy is based above all on tolerance':

> By this we mean not only the acceptance, but the welcoming, of diversity in society. This means neither indulgence nor

indifference. It can mean neutrality, if we recognise it as inactive commitment, but commitment nonetheless.

Another political attitude is an acceptance of *compromise*. There are of course other ways of resolving political differences: by war, imprisonment, censorship and other forms of force...but they are not political in the sense that we have defined it in this paper.

'Open-mindedness' is recommended as another essential political attitude in a democracy; and Bertrand Russell's advice is offered: 'When you come to a point of view maintain it with doubt.' But (the advice continues) we must not 'confuse an open mind with an empty mind'. The working paper maintains that 'some views and attitudes are arguably unacceptable in our democracy: racism, suppression of opinion, exploitation of the defenceless.' We must provide education 'which identifies the evils we must resist, and suggests how we may resist them' since, 'it is not enough ...to talk in terms of the virtues of democratic society; in addition we must provide intellectual weapons to resist those who oppose it.' The critical skills recommended are largely included in Chapter 4 of the present book, 'Language and the Curriculum' so they will not be repeated here.

Conclusion

Rights and responsibilities relating to religious observance and citizenship in a plural society have been discussed in this chapter. Some of the problems as well as the possibilities inherent in the National Curriculum have been considered. It is to be hoped that before too long a bill of rights, such as that recommended by Lord Scarman, drawing on the European Convention of Human Rights and the UN Civil and Political Rights, will provide a legal solution to some of the problems outlined. Meanwhile, educators may need reminding of the existence of the Universal Declaration of Human Rights, adopted and proclaimed by the General Assembly of the United Nations in December 1948, after which the Assembly called upon all Member countries to publicise the text of the Declaration and 'cause it to be disseminated, displayed, read and expounded principally in schools and other educational institutions, without distinction...' There may be some schools and institutions that haven't yet done this.

Chapter 8

Literature for a New World Order — (A) Principles

Who will give the human race one united system of evaluation, for evil deeds and good deeds, for the unendurable and the endurable.... I think that world literature is capable of helping the human race to understand itself properly in spite of what is being instilled into us by prejudiced people and groups....It can bring together different scales of value... and we may by this process develop a certain world vision.
(Alexander Solzhenitsyn, 1973)

Teachers should encourage wide reading, including prose, poetry, drama and non-fiction, and texts in English from other cultures and traditions.
(English for Ages 9-16, 1993, NCC Proposals)

The proper study of mankind is books. (Aldous Huxley, 1921)

The recommendation of the National Curriculum that literature should be provided which crosses cultural and national boundaries is greatly to be welcomed. This is important both for the health of our multicultural society and for enlarging our pupils' understanding of the wider world from which we can no longer isolate ourselves. Our own society is to some extent a microcosm of the 'global village' we all share, and our interdependence is steadily becoming more and more obvious — polit-ically, economically and culturally. Wisely, the revised National Curriculum still requires that from Key Stage 2 the stories, rhymes, poems and songs that the children encounter should include 'stories from a range of cultures'. English culture is in any case an amalgam of diverse sources and until a little more than a century ago its two main threads as far as literature was concerned were Classical (from Greece and Rome) and biblical from the Middle East. English literature was only grudgingly allowed into the universities in the mid-nineteenth century. Now to the advantage of our pupils we can extend their reading well beyond Europe and the Middle East to include literature (both originally in English and in translation) from Africa, the Americas, India, the Far East and the Caribbean, from all of which areas our citizens now come.

Literature has been described as 'a criticism of life' — that is to say an assessment of the human condition and different ways of living. It is also 'a celebration of life' and of the cultures which give birth to it. By encountering literature which reaches across cultural boundaries, pupils can be helped to appreciate and understand more fully the various elements — religious, linguistic, class and gender — which make up their own and others' societies. The literary exploration of interpersonal and social relations raises moral, ideological and politi-cal issues which, in discussion, can help pupils analyse problems of racism, institutional inequalities, xenophobia, etc. Inevitably such themes and concepts as diversity, similarity, justice, civilization, migration, colonialism, resistance and interdependence will arise from wide reading. Thus the broad use of literary resources recom-mended in the English programme of the National Curriculum can provide an enriching as well as a challenging and stimulating programme of reading, both for those who see their roots as lying outside the United Kingdom and those who might be tempted to imagine that the world stops at the English Channel. It is important to emphasize that this diet is recommended for all state schools, not just those in inner-city areas or communities of high multicultural concen-tration, and to all pupils. There should be no restricted access due to stereotypes of ability. Only in this way can the all-too prevalent ethnocentric historical perspectives and misrepresentations of 'alien' societies be gradually countered.

The value of imaginative literature

The National Curriculum encourages a wide range of imaginative literature in schools — 'myths, legends, fairy stories, novels, plays and poetry' — all of which serve to illuminate life by *recreating* it afresh in recognizable patterns and forms. But it is essentially *subjective* life — the world of feeling and imagination — that they are concerned to recreate. By this means our 'inner life' is given an objective embodiment, and unconscious and irrational elements of experience are brought to consciousness by what has been well described as 'imaginative reason'. Considering the place that feelings occupy in our lives — their pre-eminence in all our doings in terms of motivation, attention and response to the world around us — to ignore them, to leave them inchoate, would be to neglect a vital aspect of education. Unlike psychology or philosophy, literature does not seek to spell out analytically and discursively the nature of a feeling or emotion, or to define (for example) 'trauma', 'complex' or 'obsession'; rather it presents them to us embodied in individual characters set in situations and passing through stages of development recognizable to us as they penetrate our own dimly apprehended experience and unfold its significance to our understanding.

Imaginative literature works through ambiguity, association and suggestion, providing us with complex patterns of meanings and relationships. Because of its multiple character, each of us is able to take from it according to our own particular need of the moment. It differs from dogmatic or ideological teaching by being an *offering* rather than a rule-book or straitjacket for our thinking. Yet, from the point of view of facilitating the development of our value-systems, it is potentially more efficient since the individual must *work on it* for him or herself, evaluating the thoughts, words and actions of the various characters and their interactions, assessing these things in the light of their consequences within the work itself and in relation to the reader's own experiences. This process may be conscious or unconscious, but in either case it is a process motivated from *within* and not imposed by external authority.

Our response to imaginative literature is clearly a very personal matter and will depend upon our individual purposes. In a multi-cultural classroom a teacher may have to be aware of a variety of highly charged expectations and needs. African, Caribbean or Indian literature, for example, may have a special meaning for individuals or groups who are the victims of prejudice, institutional racism or xeno-phobia. For them such material may be the means of confirming their sense of identity and developing and asserting aspects of their cultural background. For others the encounter may simply be the means of extending their knowledge of, and sensitivity towards, another culture; and the pleasure derived will be from extending the breadth of their experience and the depth of their understanding.

In both cases there is likely to be an increase in *self-knowledge*, and it is probably true to say that the more complex a society becomes and the more potentially bewildering the external world seems, the more vital does this become for the individual. To be a member of a minority group surrounded by a host of more or less suspicious neighbours and to be a member of the indigenous group feeling threatened by the presence of new and 'alien' neighbours are different experiences, but potentially they have certain elements in common: a fear of the 'other-ness' of one's neighbour; some risk of a crisis of personal and social identity; a tendency to seek for group solidarity; a readiness to rationalize anxieties by stereotyping and to exercise aggressive impulses by scape-goating. All or none of these characteristics may feature in specific situations within a multicultural society, but they indicate something of the range of possibilities. The need to promote a secure sense of identity and raise the self-confidence of individuals is evident. By its inwardness good literature can help establish self-awareness; by its honest delineation of a human being's moral com-plexity and diversity of motivation it can help us come to terms with our negative side, our *shadow*, without loss of self-respect; and by its confident exposition of paradox, irony, doubt and tentativeness it can help reduce the need for the uncritical dogmatic assertiveness that tends to accompany fear of the bewildering or unknown. The facilitat-ing of a faculty for empathy with others, in their different situations, is an equally important function of literature. And perhaps even more important is the capacity of literature to help cultivate confident tolerance of uncertainty and diversity. To feel at ease in a state of tentativeness, doubt and 'provisional belief' is to be at home in the 'real' world with all its complexities and alternative viewpoints held generally in good faith by others with whom we have to co-exist and cooperate.

Literature in English from Commonwealth and so-called 'New Commonwealth' countries is inevitably marked by idioms, vocabulary and variations of style which are more or less unfamiliar to readers fed solely on a diet of 'mainstream' English. Caribbean poetry, in particular, for example, may be expressed partly or entirely in Creole which, in the words of Suzanne Scafe (1989), 'continues to be developed, revalued and celebrated by writers and speakers who deliberately foster its use, both as a subversive means of communication and as an open, legitimate expression of cultural unity'. Developed partly as a language of convenience, it also has symbolic value because of its 'historic functions of resistance and subversion'. Students who appreciate this will not make the mistake of treating material in Creole as 'low status', but will interpret and assess it on its own merits. The National Curriculum (in its first draft) recognized this explicitly in its requirement that 'pupils should be encouraged to respect their own language(s) or dialect(s) and those of others'. We must assume that it remains implicit in the revised Proposals despite the emphasis on the acquisition of standard English. For some pupils Creole prose and poetry will be an expression authenticating their own identity; for others it will have the merit of freshness and novelty, providing a challenge to their powers of deduction, imagination and interpretation. In either case it can be the means of increasing understanding of one's own culture and that of others.

The value of wide reading

Nothing of what has been said is intended to devalue the importance of 'mainstream' literature which has an obvious and secure place in the curriculum. An earlier draft of the National Curriculum rightly challenged the self-sufficiency of an established 'canon' of works, but a later Order has virtually created one! However, the wording of the new lists provided has sensibly avoided being totally prescriptive: it refers to 'categories' of literature, and the lists (headed by 'such as...') are evidently meant to be examples. In each case, moreover, there is at least one example from a non-European source. The offerings, therefore, must necessarily be regarded as suggestions: no self-respecting teachers of literature would in any case allow their own or their pupils' horizons to be bounded by prescribed lists — lists which will in any case be modified by future revisions.

To provide an adequate diet of literature, a balance has to be struck between indigenous and non-native literature now available in English if the next generation is to be equipped to understand their social, political and economic environment with any degree of success. The problems of the late twentieth and the coming twenty-first century cannot be addressed by a generation of minds straitjac-keted with 'fixed ideas'. Even membership of the European Com-munity will make demands on increasing flexibility of social adjustment and understanding, which European literature in trans-lation can help develop. But Eurocentricism is not enough: literature of the 'developed' and 'developing' countries of the Commonwealth, of the Americas, of India and Japan — all has its place in widening horizons and deepening consciousness of our shared humanity and global responsibilities. A Unesco Resolution at its 22nd General Conference in 1983 reflected 'a widespread concern to ensure that languages and literatures of developing countries are more widely read and appreciated *as part of the cultural heritage of humanity*' and sought 'to improve the balance of international cultural relations and exchanges' in order 'to foster better international understanding and the flow of information on cultures between all nations'.

Over a century ago the great Victorian educationist, Matthew Arnold (1869), recognized the value of a broad-based culture.

> Plenty of people (he wrote) will try to indoctrinate the masses with the set of ideas and judgments constituting the creed of their own profession or party....But culture works differently: It seeks to do away with classes; *to make the best that has been thought and known in the world current everywhere;* to make all men live in an atmosphere of sweetness and light, where they may use ideas, as it uses them itself, freely — nourished, and not bound by them. This is the social idea; and the men of culture are the true apostles of equality.'

No one can deny that there still remains a lack of 'sweetness and light' (that is to say, of 'sensitivity and understanding') in present-day inter-cultural and international relations that needs redressing. But matters can be improved. Readers who range widely, even within a single language, cannot help becoming aware of the diverse nature of their own society and the cultural variety which is the product of its own history and contacts with other cultures. Moreover, a reader with wide interests and sensitivities quickly becomes aware of the contrast-ing angles on ideas and experience which are available from writers whose sex, class allegiance, or cultural background differ from those which dominate the mainstream of available literary works. Such readers are inclined already towards the opportunities which the availability of texts from less well-known national literatures offer and welcome access to learning about other cultures and experiences. The resultant reading is reciprocal in its effects, providing the reader with ways of interpreting his or her own culture at the same time as experiencing other views of the world. Fortunately, the standard of contemporary literature in English coming from beyond the British Isles is extremely high — Nobel Prizewinners for literature and winners of the Booker Prize can be numbered among writers from Africa, Asia and the Caribbean. So there is no excuse for avoiding non-mainstream literature on the grounds of quality.

If for no other reason than exposing to ourselves our own unconscious ethnocentrity, insularity and xenophobia, this broadened diet is to be welcomed. As Alastair Niven (1987) writes:

> ...fifteen years ago...textbooks in schools still spoke of Columbus and Livingstone 'discovering' the 'New World' and the 'Victoria Falls' as though these places had no existence and no local names before them, of Africa as a history-less continent before the arrival of the white man and of the 'dawn of civilization' rising in Greece and Egypt, without reference to the Indian and sub-Saharan culture from which Greece and Egypt drew.

Even some of the 'best' of mainstream writing is tainted in places with unconscious racism and Chauvinism. One needn't go as far as Kipling or Rupert Brooke to find this. In the otherwise excellent, sensitive and progressive work of Laurens Van der Post — a pioneer in seeking better understanding between North and South and East and West, and a valuable interpreter of Jung — there remain involuntary traces of racism in the assumption that African chiefs should inevitably find teams of 'bearers' at a moment's notice for white explorers and in characterisations of the 'noble savage' or the dependent 'native'. Such connotations — which happily are reduced in his later work — only become apparent after wider reading and the comparative perspective that this facilitates.

What is 'national culture'?

When questions of widening our reading horizons come up, some people express anxiety about the possible erosion of 'our national heritage' of literature and the destabilization of our shared culture. And this is understandable. Points of reference held in common give us a sense of security. We can make allusions and know that we shall by understood. But it is an illusion to think that literary culture is a static phenomenon. The Latin quotations that were a feature of much nineteenth century writing have disappeared today without a great deal of regret from most people. (The majority were in any case excluded from sharing in these allusions.) And the puns that might have

Mohandas K. Gandhi (1869-1948)

A social reformer and moral leader, Gandhi's advocacy of non-violent civil disobedience played a major part in the movement for India's independence. Throughout his life he strove against injustice and dscrimination and sought to promote cooperation between black and white and between followers of different faiths. He was not convinced that 'western civilisation' was entirley 'a good thing'.

delighted Shakespeare's audiences tend to fall rather flat in the theatre today (despite the abundant annotations of a host of Shakespearean text editors). With several thousand new books of fiction and poetry appearing every year in the United Kingdom alone, the English literary heritage is under constant forces of modification and renewal. It is surely not unreasonable to wish that the flow should take account of a changing population.

Is a national culture what boosts and props up the state? Or what unites a people? Or what issues from a given language? Totalitarian countries have tried the first course, and it is always doomed to failure. Germans now again read literature by German Jews (forbidden under the Third Reich), and former *samizdat* is now popular and legitimate reading in Russia. People are probably best united by rejoicing in their variety. Human beings are not clones — not yet, at least. Fortunately the flexibility of the English language and the range of its distribution means that we probably have the broadest heritage in the world. Our membership of Europe, in addition, gives us an extension of our cultural range through literature in translation, if not always in the original. Our membership of the Commonwealth offers exceptional scope for insight into new literary settings and experiences. But most important of all, is our membership of humanity, so that gradually, if only through translations, we can come to know those things that are universal and important to the human condition, to living life fully and turning away from the destructive paths that blinkered, insular thinking has so often lead to.

As an experiment to test out what might be considered to represent a sort of 'canon' of 'national' English literary culture I consulted the *Oxford Dictionary of English Quotations* (3rd.Edition, 1980). The 1st Edition (1930) was said to have been compiled 'by men and women imbued with... the culture whether educated or popular of the first quarter of twentieth century Britain'. The 3rd edition was to bring it up to date, with 'taste and discrimination' and a measure of 'aptness and truth', although inclusion is admitted to be on 'popularity and not merit'. I forgive Shakespeare his 2000-odd quotations — he is eminently quotable, and many of his expressions have passed into everyday English language. But among more recent writers quoted there was a notable lack of proportion. Kipling, for example, has 203 quotations, W.S. Gilbert 141, Martin Luther King 2 and M K Gandhi (whose influence in modern times is not negligible!) nil. Gandhi is by no means

Rudyard Kipling (1865-1936)
Nobel Prizewinner for Literature (1907), Kipling's work vividly portrays contemporary British rule in India where he was born. His works, notably Kim *and* The Jungle Book, *are recommended reading in the English programme of the National Curriculum. However, they should be used (if at all) with care. They are almost inevitably marred by a strong, if unconscious, streak of racism. Indians, along with beasts of burden, are clearly 'Her Majesty's Servants' (and the Viceroy's) in the last chapter of* The *Jungle Book, and the kind of obedience to be exacted brings to mind the significance of the Nurenburg Trials.*

unquotable: Indian diaries printed in English find a quotation for every day of the year. The *Penguin Book of Modern Quotations* (1983) tends to follow the Oxford book's priorities: Kipling has 92 quotations, Greta Garbo two and Gandhi one. However, the *Sphere Handbook of Twentieth Century Quotations* (1984) finds space for twelve quotations by Gandhi and seven about him, and has only ten by Kipling. This seems a healthy change.

I have laboured this point because familiarity doesn't always breed contempt: in prestigious books of reference it more often breeds yet more familiarity. Kipling has written much that is interesting and worthwhile, but not all of it quoted in the *Oxford Dictionary of Quotations* is helpful today. For instance:

> Take up the White Man's burden —
>> Send forth the best ye breed —
> Go, bind your sons to exile
>> To serve your captives' need;
> To wait in heavy harness
>> On fluttered folk and wild —
> Your new-caught, sullen peoples
>> Half-devil and half-child.

If this is to be part of our ongoing heritage — perhaps 'the culture of the first quarter of the twenty-first century'? — then maybe there is need for some modification. I recognize that books of quotations aim to provide a record of memorable things that have been said and written, and do not have to confine themselves to the 'best' things that have been said and written. But perhaps the *Oxford Dictionary of Quotations* could strive a little harder to achieve a balance among selected utterances in the English language. From Gandhi, for example:

> I am not conscious of a single experience throughout my three months stay in England and Europe that made me feel that after all East is East and West is West. On the contrary, I have been convinced more than ever that human nature is much the same, no matter under what clime it flourishes, and that if you approached people with trust and affection you would have ten-fold trust and thousand-fold affection returned to you.

Or the more pithy: 'There is enough for the needy, but not for the greedy.' Once when asked what he thought about western civilization, Gandhi replied: 'I think it would be a good idea!' Perhaps it would be a good idea for ideas on our cultural inheritance to catch up with the times.

It might be suggested that Gandhi was excluded from the *Oxford Dictionary of Quotations* because he was not English. However, a quick glance reveals eight quotations from Conrad (Polish), 25 from Mark Twain (American), and eleven from Lucretius (Roman). Perhaps the most charitable word for this kind of bias is 'Eurocentrism', but I could think of others.

A national culture, or literary 'inheritance', does not depend upon the products of conformist writers. The sacred writings of the Jews are full of criticisms of the 'establishment': the prophets criticized their rulers mercilessly whether the latter were Jewish or not. And in English literature William Blake, Dean Swift and George Bernard Shaw are among many who are highly critical of the state. Much literature — particularly satire, and many poems, novels and plays — aims either directly or indirectly to improve society by their criticism. Rightly, in its lists, the revised English Proposals recognize that it would be unfortunate for pupils in English schools to leave without having encountered some of the poetry of Siegfried Sassoon and Wilfren Owen. (Incidentally, I must give the *Oxford Dictionary of Quotations* credit for making space for them.) The haunting poem 'Strange Meeting', with its eloquent testimony to 'the truth untold / the pity of war', is worth its place in any curriculum. It opens with a dreamlike passage:

> It seemed that out of battle I escaped
> Down some profound dull tunnel...

where the dreamer finds himself in Hell, face to face with his victim of the previous day. The spectre mourns 'the undone years' and 'the hopelessness' of their situation. 'Whatever hope was yours,' he reminds his unwilling slayer, 'Was my life also.' In happier circumstances, he says:

> I would have poured my spirit without stint
> But not through wounds; not on the cess of war.

The poem concludes with the memorable lines spoken by the victim:

> ...I am the enemy you killed, my friend.
> I knew you in this dark: for so you frowned
> Yesterday through me as you jabbed and killed.
> I parried; but my hands were loath and cold.
> Let us sleep now....

'Dulce Et Decorum Est' deals equally poignantly with the horrors of a gas attack, concentrating on the plight of one of its victims. Its bitter conclusion focuses once again on the pointlessness of war:

> If in some smothering dreams you too could pace
> Behind the wagon that we flung him in...
> My friend, you would not tell with such high zest
> To children ardent for some despearate glory,
> The old Lie: Dulce et decorum est
> Pro patria mori.

These poems and, for example, 'The Parable of the Old Man and the Young', are samples of the many writings of that period that show that national literature does not have to be national*istic* literature. They should certainly be included somewhere in the English curriculum as part of the heritage of mankind. Maybe the time for thinking in terms of a 'national heritage' is now past, anyway.

Close reading and contextual awareness

In addition to requiring 'wide reading', the National Curriculum also requires 'close reading' — the analysis of printed material 'with some degree of sophistication'. It encourages readers 'to compare surface meanings in a text with an implied sub-text' and warns students to be aware of 'the difference between attitudes or assumptions displayed by a character and those of an author'. Students are to explore 'conflicting points of view' and to be helped to handle the elements 'of a story which involves characters in very different contexts' (Attainment Target Three). All this is to be welcomed as a valuable contribution to breaking down rigidity of thinking and encouraging critical attitudes.

It is not always easy to separate an author from his or her characters. In Alan Sillitoe's *The Loneliness of the Long-distance Runner*, for example, how much of the Borstal boy's attitudes and behaviour does Sillitoe condone? Presumably he admires his courage, resilience and determination, but does not recommend burglary as a means of livelihood (after all, he has chosen to be an author himself!). At the same time Sillitoe sympathizes with Joe's circumstances, understands the reasons for his alienation and is critical of the hypocritical and repressive establishment that holds him down. I have chosen this example because it is a relatively straightforward one. In a multicultural inner-city classroom where many pupils (like the long-distance runner) may have reason to feel alienated and bitter towards the establishment and towards their lot in life, the teacher has a delicate task in guiding them through material of this kind. A good deal of commonwealth, post-colonial, literature is concerned with protest and struggle against inequalities and injustices in national and international economic and political arrangements. How can pupils be helped to understand these things and inspired to work for desirable changes without being encouraged to seek violent and counterproductive means to the desired ends? I shall not attempt to answer this; it is intended as a challenge rather than a question! But unless material which questions and protests against the *status quo* is introduced into the classroom, there is no chance that students will learn to appreciate alternative points of view and to seek for the solution of conflicts. In a given classroom there is likely to be a wide range of opinion, and it is useful to provide texts which are *obliquely* relevant to the pupils' own lives upon which they can exercise their views and arguments.

There is a danger that some teachers might introduce 'Third World' literature as a 'sop' to black pupils, and this must be strenuously resisted. Whatever material is studied must be examined with rigour. As Suzanne Scafe (1989) puts the matter:

> The task for teachers and educationalists is to ensure that Black writing is valued critically, that it is read as it defines itself, as a cultural and artistic whole reflecting and a reflection of the political and cultural struggles which are its context. The reading should not be used to confirm its status as 'other' but to 'change the perceptions' of the minority who are the gate-keepers of the canon and who have defined 'human' in terms of their own image.

In other words mainstream Shakespeare and Nigerian novels or Caribbean Anansi Spider stories should be subject to the same critical close reading and their underlying values considered.

Just as historical context must be taken into account in studying Shakespeare's plays or Defoe's novels, so it is relevant in considering the writing of Achebe, Schweitzer or *The Qur'an*. The traces of racism and paternalism in the otherwise valuable writings of Schweitzer or Laurens Van der Post; the rigour and harshness in parts of the *Qur'an*; and the superstition described by Achebe can all be better understood in terms of their context. Seen as products of a given time and circumstances they can be read with more sensitivity to their author's intentions. The exercise of students' critical faculties is given a fresh impetus and a wider scope by the introduction of more varied texts into the curriculum. In the words of Alastair Niven(1986):

> How can a student approach *Hamlet* or *Pride and Prejudice* with the freshness that is still possible when he encounters contemporary works from unfamiliar backgrounds that do not have a weight of critical barnacles clinging to them?

Principles of choice*

In looking for literature to promote intercultural and international understanding the problem is not one of availability but of selection. So it may be helpful to provide some ground-rules here before listing a number of examples in the next chapter:

1. Obviously material must be suitable for the age-range and ability of the pupils concerned. But from Key Stage 1 to Key Stage 4 there is no problem here. There is an abundance of non-Eurocentric rhymes, fairy stories and folktales for the youngest children and of novels, philosophical works, drama, biography, etc, for the oldest and most advanced. There is also plenty of material illustrating examples of conflict and conflict resolution at levels appropriate to a wide range of pupils' understanding.

2. Material should promote the *personal* development of pupils both as individuals and as members of the communities and societies to which they belong. It should help them towards an awareness of belonging to an interdependent world community where sensitivity to the experience of others (with the *felt* realization of the special nature of others' experiences that literature can help to provide) can be a means of breaking down the artificial barriers which separate communities from one another.

3. The literature chosen should to some extent mirror the pupils' sense of identity and support their self-understanding and self-esteem.

4. It should promote their linguistic development as speakers and writers, making them aware of new possibilities of what can be thought or expressed.

5. It should further their imagination and emotional development, enabling them to project themselves into the lives, attitudes and concerns of members of other races, cultures and communities.

6. It should increase their respect for, understanding of and interest in different points of view, and the perspectives of other peoples.

7. As a result of their reading pupils should be made aware of the dynamic nature of cultures and communities and thus be freed from the myth of society as a static entity.

8. It should illuminate their understanding of history, religion and the humanities by providing evidence of new perspectives.

9. Access should be provided to the literary heritage of both majority and minority cultures for the sake of balance.

---

* These principles incorporate material from Jagdish Gundara (1987) for which I am much indebted.

10. Some of the material should focus on the interaction of different cultures (including examples of conflict, contrast, similarity and the universality of the human experience) to help pupils face up to racism and prejudice and seek their elimination.

11. It should foster the production of new writing and literature expressing experiences and showing understanding of the viewpoints of minorities within particular communities.

12. The experience of intercultural and international literature should provide a platform for carrying these views and values into the wider world to change it for the better.

There is nothing in the National Curriculum to prevent schools and teachers putting these principles into practice; neither is there any shortage of suitable material. The major problems will probably be resources for the library and class readers, and ensuring that time is made available to do justice to the possibilities.

Chapter 9

Literature for a New World Order (B) — A Range of Material

The reading material provided should include a range of fiction, non-fiction and poetry, as well as periodicals....These should include works written in English from other cultures. School and class libraries should provide as wide a range as possible....folk tales and fables might include translations from original sources...
(English in the National Curriculum, DES, p.30)

...a balance...needs to be struck between the reading of, on the one hand, English and, on the other, commonwealth and world literature.
(English for ages 5-16, 1993, NCC Proposals)

National literature is now rather an unmeaning term: the epoch of world literature is at hand, and everyone must strive to hasten its approach.
(J W Goethe, Conversations with Eckerman, 1827)

This is a chapter of suggestions. I found, much to my pleasure, that quite a number of the suggestions made in an earlier draft of the following pages (both of specific books and of authors) also figure in the lists since recommended in the revised English Proposals. Also encouraging was the emphasis I found in the Proposals on reading as 'an enjoyable activity' aiming to 'stimulate pupils' imagination and enthusiasm'. I hope the following offerings will be found to be fully in line with this aim.

The problem of classification arises here. Should it be according to *genre* (prose, poetry, drama, folk-tales, etc); or theme (books for minority groups; development literature; conflict resolution, etc); or source of material (Africa, Europe, India, etc)? After piling up several hundred books, it seemed best to opt for age-suitability, although of course divisions of this kind are necessarily arbitrary and must be handled flexibly to cope with children of varied abilities and interests.

a. Younger children (Key Stage One)

In addition to requiring literature covering 'a range of stimulating texts, both fiction and non-fiction' and 'including stories from a variety of cultures', the original National Curriculum specified that 'reading should include picture books, nursery rhymes, poems, folk-tales, myths, legends and other literature *which takes account of pupils' linguistic competences and backgrounds*' and which builds on 'the oral language and experiences which pupils bring from home'. Thus all children's horizons are to be enlarged, but at the same time provision must be made for children in minority groups to meet material with which they are familiar or with which they can readily identify both linguistically and in terms of their experience. The omission of this emphasis in the revised Proposals is disappointing; but teachers will obviously still use their discretion and apply what remains a valid principle where they think fit.

Rowena Akinyemi's *A Hole in the Hedge* and *Hamster Weekend* (Hamish Hamilton, 1992), both suitable for beginner readers, portray with warmth and simplicity the life of a Nigerian family in England where the three children settle down to life in their new home and in their multiracial, multicultural school. Also dealing with domestic adjustment is *Home* by Kamala Nair (1967) — a delightful picture book illustrated by K.S. Kulkarni. Published in India by the Children's Book Trust, its meaning and message are universal, including such ideas as 'Neighbours can at times be a little frightening...' but 'if you welcome them with a warm smile they will be nice to you and you are no longer afraid of them'. Fear of being different and of isolation is dealt with in a number of children's picture books. *Crow Boy*, a Picture Puffin by Taro Yashima, tells of a shy, frightened boy, scorned by classmates, who eventually makes good by his special skill in imitating crows. Set in Japan the language has a few unproblemmatical Americanisms such as 'graduating' from an elementary school and being finally 'honored' (in American spelling). *Whistle for Willie*, a Puffin Picture Book by Ezra Jack Keats, is one of many British publications featuring black schoolchildren, that have for some time been available in England. In this case the hero learns through much effort to overcome his inability to whistle. *The Trouble with Mum* by Babette Cole (1983) deals delightfully with another childhood problem — anxiety about the presentability of a parent. Here, although the mother in question is something of an oddity — a witch with extraordinary and alarming powers — she eventually wins over the other parents and neighbours by saving the school from a fire! A lively, wide-ranging selection of poems from Black, Asian and Amerindian cultures, suitable for young readers, is *Can I Buy a Slice of Sky?* (Blackie,1992) edited by Grace Nichols and illustrated by Liz Thomas. Its themes are school, play, the world at large, love and people, and in dealing with these it seeks to emphasise similarities as much as differences.

Wilfred Owen (1893-1918)
Owen is justly included among recommended reading in the English programme of the National Curriculum. His have been described as 'probably the greatest poems about war in our literature'. In a Preface to a book of his poems he wrote:

> *This book is not about heroes. English poetry is not yet fit to speak of them.*
> *Nor is it about deeds, or lands, nor anything about glory, honour, might, majesty, dominion, or power, except War.*
> *Above all I am not concerned with Poetry.*
> *My subject is War, and the pity of War.*
> *The poetry is in the pity.*
> *Yet these elegies are to this generation in no sense consolatory, they may be to the next. All a poet can do today is warn...*

Owen himself was killed at 25 in the last phase of World War I.

An interesting development which deserves cautious but positive approval is the publication by the Blackfriars Settlement Literacy Scheme of a child's own account of her Jamaican childhood. *Muriel's Book* (Peckham Publishing Project, 1978) is entirely in her own words. The spelling is standard, but the idiom being mildly West Indian, ('My mother make me a doll and dress' and 'She buy me a little slate and book'), would be familiar to West Indian children and a little less daunting to them in the early stages of reading than some standard texts might be.

On questions of war and conflict suitably adapted for young children Michael Foreman has produced some very interesting and colourful books in the Picture Puffin series. *Moose* features a peace-loving animal caught up between the name-calling and violence of Bear and Eagle. He shows finally how their destructive weapons of sticks and stones can be put to more creative use. In *War and Peas* he tackles the problem of the unequal distribution of wealth. A brave but emaciated lion seeks help for his famished people in the land of the Fat King. The latter refuses to help 'beggars' and attacks the lion's people. His aggression misfires, however, peace is restored, and finally it is found that there is 'plenty for everyone!' Michael Foreman produces a further colourful and light-hearted, but meaningful critique, this time related to environmental pollution in *Dinosaurs and all that Rubbish* where scientific and technological development is shown not to be value-free because 'the earth belongs to everyone' and is not to be despoiled for the sake of individual greed and selfishness.

A colourful book which deals skilfully with both sexism and racism is Mary Hoffman's *Amazing Grace* (1992). The black heroine, Grace, proves her 'amazing' determination by overcoming all obstacles in order to play the part of Peter Pan in the school play. Family support and positive self-image play an important role in the story. The illustrations by Caroline Binch add to the charm of this popular book. Also dealing with sexism is Irene Hedlund's *Mighty Mountain and the Three Strong Women* (1984), a story set in Japan in which a would-be 'macho' strong man is amusingly tamed by his encounters with the opposite sex to end up usefully employed as a farmer. And still popular with younger pupils are: *The Faithful Parrot and Other Indian Folk Tales* by Taya Zinkin (OUP,1968), *Come Over to My House* by Theo Le Sieg (Collins, 1967), *Jonothan and Large*, by Rosemary Grimble (Deutsch, 1965), *Taresh the Tea Planter* and *No Mules* by William Papas (OUP, 1968), *Folk Tales of the World: India* edited by A.W.Crown (Arnold, 1963) and a number of books by Ezra Jack Keats.

(b) Upper primary age-range (Key Stage Two)

Again the 'range of fiction, non-fiction and poetry' offered is to include 'works written in English from other cultures', but now the pupils 'should be encouraged to develop their personal taste in reading with guidance from the teacher and to become more independent and reflective'. They should also 'hear stories, non-fiction and poems read aloud' to them which opens the possibility of encountering some rather more difficult material which a skilful teacher can adapt and interpret to meet their needs and abilities. Well-told myths and legends still have a special appeal, and those of ancient Greece are no exception: the exploits of Hercules and of Perseus, for example. To these can now be added *Myths and Legends of Africa* (Margaret Carey, Hamlyn 1970) and an equally colourful companion volume *Myths and Legends of India* (Veronica Ions, Hamlyn 1970) and *Tales of Ancient Egypt* (Roger Lancelyn Green, Penguin 1970), among many others. While there is a universally appealing quality about most myths and legends which easily crosses cultural boundaries, there is also a considerable diversity in the way myths from different cultures approach the 'explanation' of origins of the world, the elements, humankind and good and evil. This diversity can be a healthy antidote to rigid and dogmatic thinking based on the particular explanations offered in the early records of the experience of the different world religions. *In the Beginning: Creation Stories from Around the World* (1982) deals with this theme. It is a fascinating collection of twenty-five myths from Egypt, China, Eskimo and North American peoples, Greek mythology and the Bible, etc, sympathetically retold by Virginia Hamilton and beautifully illustrated by Barry Moser.

While myths tend to be the constructions of the learned and priestly classes in society and legends very often (but not always) tend to extol the heroic exploits of the great and famous, folk tales by their very nature generally come from the other end of the social spectrum. Thus they delight in the cunning and guile of the little man or woman, and applaud ways in which the underdog gets the better of his would-be 'superiors' and oppressors. Often amoral by higher ethical standards, they nevertheless provide a healthy boost to the morale of the underprivileged in society, offering the satisfaction of seeing power and dignity knocked off their perch. The Ananse tales from Ghana come into this category. *In Tales of an Ashanti Father* (1967) and *The Pineapple Child and Other Tales from Ashanti* (both by Peggy Appiah, Deutsch 1967 & 1969, respectively), Ananse the spider-man proves himself a tough and amusing adversary to the bigger and stronger creatures he encounters in his adventures. He turns up again in the West Indies as *Anansi the Spider Man* (Philip M Sherlock, Macmillan, 1956) or sometimes as Anancy, where in the Jamaican slave culture his resillience must have been of particular value to the morale of the oppressed slave community. Kalulu the crafty rabbit hero fulfils a similar function in many African stories.

Of the many stories featuring speaking animals among human beings *Charlotte's Web* is surely one of the most endearing and salutary in its values. In this tale of a pig rescued by a spider, E.B.White (Puffin, 1963) has managed to create animal characters who are both tough and, when appropriate, tender. The story copes superbly with problems of loneliness, conflict, violence in nature and death. Wilbur, the lonely pig, is shocked when he finds that his new friend, Charlotte, drinks the blood of her victims with evident relish. But the spider explains:

> I am not entirely happy about my diet of flies and bugs, but it's the way I'm made. A spider has to pick up a living somehow or other, and I happen to be a trapper. I just naturally build a web and trap flies and other insects. My mother was a trapper before me.... All our family have been trappers. Way back for thousands of years we spiders have been laying for flies and bugs.

In response to Wilbur's criticism, 'It's cruel', Charlotte explains: '...do you realise that if I didn't catch bugs and eat them, bugs would increase and multiply and get so numerous that they'd destroy the earth, wipe out everything?' Despite this lesson in ecology, Wilbur undergoes 'the doubts and fears that often go with finding a new friend'! But through many adventures and much help from Charlotte, Wilbur's admiration for Charlotte ripens, and when she finally dies he is overcome with grief. In an episode which is handled with both lyricism and toughness he comes to terms with her stoical acceptance of death and helps to secure the safety of her numerous offspring, which brings both him and the reader final satisfaction.

The Kaziranga Trail (Arup Kumar Datta, Children's Book Trust New Delhi,1979), is another adventure involving animals, but of a different kind. Two young boys are the heroes of this eventful naturalistic tale set in the Kazaringa wild life sanctuary where the basically harmless rhinoceros is illegally hunted for profit by cruel poachers who will stop at nothing to gain their ends. The underlying theme of environmental protection neither intrudes nor detracts from the cliff-hanging excitement of the story. Among other stories in which young people in different parts of the world are caught up in the world of adults are a

Perseus Slaying the Three-headed Monster
This drawing — the response of an eight-year-old to the story of Perseus — is clear evidence that the ancient Greek myths still have a hold on the imagination of the young. The use of myths and legends from around the world is encouraged in the National Curriculum.

number with strong anti-war and anti-violence themes. The most recent, perhaps, is Elizabeth Lutzeier's *The Wall* (Oxford, 1991), a moving story about life in former East Berlin where the heroine, Hannah, learns to hide her feelings when her mother is shot. Going back in time, *The Silver Sword* by Ian Serraillier (Jonathan Cape, 1956) tells of four Polish children who make their way across war-torn Europe to find their parents. *The House of Sixty Fathers* (Meindert DeJong, Penguin, 1966), set in China also in the Second World War, shows the courage of a young Chinese boy, separated from his parents, who survives numerous trials before he is finally reunited with his family. Lettice Cooper's *Twig of Cypress* (Deutsch, 1965) features a boy caught up in Garibaldi's unification of Italy. And *The Devil's Children* by Peter Dickinson (Gollancz, 1970) deals with the problems of xenophobia faced by a travelling community of Sikhs who have to cope with hostility and danger in an England that has reverted to medieval times.

Communication problems of a different kind occur in *Stig of the Dump* (Clive King, Penguin, 1963) and *Walkabout* (James Vance Marshall,

Penguin, 1963). Barney, in *Stig of the Dump*, has to communicate with someone who has somehow survived from the stone age and cannot speak his language; and the book also includes the use of different dialects, which provides an opening for consideration of 'standard' and 'non-standard' English. In any case, this story about friendship and overcoming fear of the unknown is worth reading for its own sake. *Walkabout* presents the clash of two widely different cultures when an aboriginal Australian boy saves two western children from exhaustion and death through his helpfulness and skill in finding nourishment and his knowledge of pathfinding in a harsh environment. The preconditioning and prejudice of the Western girl, Mary, prevents her from accepting and recognising the full humanity of the aboriginal boy, until very near the end of the story when he dies:

> It was (his) smile that broke Mary's heart: that last forgiving smile. Before, she had seen through a glass darkly, but now she saw face to face. And in that moment of truth all her inbred fears and inhibitions were sponged away, and she saw that the world which she had thought was split in two was one.

Two stories which in different ways help to put a new perspective on our small shared globe spinning in space are H.G. Wells' short story *Under the Knife* and the French *The Little Prince* by Antoine de Saint-Exupery. I have found it useful to abridge the Wells story when telling it to upper primary school children. It tell of a man near death under an operation whose soul travels out of his body and steadily moves out into space, focusing as it goes on his town, the countryside, his country surrounded by the sea, Europe, the earth floating in space and finally the whole glory of interstellar space. Returning to consciousness after the successful operation, the man has a new concept of the meaning of life. *The Little Prince* (Penguin translation,1962) tells of a stranded pilot's encounter with a charming humanoid being from another minuscule planet. The values that emerge as the Little Prince space-hops from one fantastic asteroid to another are of tenderness, humility and concern for the environment. While on the subject of fantasy in international literature, *Pinocchio* by Carlo Collodi (Dent,1976), is probably the best and most humane story of a puppet ever written. A new version of this, vigorously retold by James Riordan (Oxford Educational, 1992) and colourfully illustrated by Victor Ambrus, may be worth considering for the school library.

Far from fantasy is the all-too-true-to-life *Journey to Jo'burg* by Beverly Naidoo (1985) written 'in memory of two small children who died far away from their mother...who worked in Jo'burg'. Fortunately, this story is given a happy ending despite the many obstacles that two brave South African children have to overcome in order to find their mother and bring her home from her workplace to look after an ill sister. The injustices of apartheid are skilfully introduced into the narrative and so is the courage of those determined to oppose it and work for a changed society. The words of a children's playground song are telling:

> Beware that policeman
> He'll want to see your 'pass'
> He'll say it's not in order,
> That day may be your last!

And the reality of the situation is borne out when the children have their first experience of the big city where arrests are made, buses are segregated and an atmosphere of violence prevails. Real photographs of life in South Africa conclude the book — dramatically illustrating the contrasts. Despite all the realism in the book, however, the overall impression left is positive, optimistic and heartwarming.

Finally, some mention of biography is appropriate for this age-group who like to know the stories of grown-ups' lives but who have hither-to been fed largely on a diet of colonisers and battle-heroes. There is a need to learn about lives of courageous men and women whose achievements were for humanity at large and without Chauvinistic overtones. Approp-priate biographies can be found of Elizabeth Fry, Florence Nightingale, Helen Keller, Louis Braille, Gandhi, Martin Luther King, Pierre Ceresole, Nelson Mandela, Tolstoi, Pasteur and many others who have made positive contributions to human happi-ness, as of international musicians, artists, writers and philanthropists. Bravery in face of oppression and suffering is chronicled in Ann McGovern's biography of Harriet Tubman, who masterminded the Underground Railroad enabling slaves in South-ern American states to escape to the North. Esteban Montejo's *Auto-biography of a Runaway Slave*, a Cuban slave who emerged from his experiences without bitterness, can provide extracts, at least, which can be read to upper primary children. Experiences of childhood are also useful for this age-group. For example Shankar's *Life with Grand-father* (Children's Book Trust, New Delhi, 1965) provides amusing reminiscences from the life of an Indian boy. *Jason Whyte, Jamaican* by Terry Parris (OUP,1973) chronicles the true, exciting and frightening adventures of a West Indian boy stranded at sea in an open boat but eventually rescued and reunited with his parents. The ILEA English Centre published a brief but interesting account of the life of a

Moroccan boy, Mohammed Elbaja, written when he was in the fifth form at school *My Life* (English Centre, 1978). While not 'great literature' this 16-page pamphlet is an honest and quite moving account of the experience of displacement with which many primary school pupils in multicultural classrooms could identify. This, together with similar accounts of the lives of other London school-children with Chinese, Irish, Ugandan and other origins, can still be read in *Our Lives: Young People's Autobiographies* (English and Media Centre, 1979).

(c) Secondary school years (Key Stages three and four)

The revised Proposals for English in the National Curriculum require that:

> During these key stages, pupils should read a wide variety of literature and other texts....They should be encouraged to read independently solely for enjoyment. The texts should be pro-gressively more demanding and introduce pupils to the literary heritage....The range of texts should include: a variety of genres, including poetry, novels, plays and short stories (and) texts from other cultures and traditions...'

Some of the material discussed in the previous section will be suitable for younger secondary school pupils; but at this stage, as divisions of ability and maturity begin to get wider, there will be some eleven and twelve year olds who will be ready to tackle adult literature.

Among stories suitable at the middle school stage is another one deal-ing with the realities of South Africa: Sheila Gordon's *Waiting for the Rain* (Orchard, 1988). It deals with the friendship of a gifted black boy eager for education and a white boy impatient to become a farmer. The grim circumstances of their environment gradually force the friends into opposing camps. Less sober, but equally compassionate, is the story of another black and white friendship, this time set in England. *The Runaways* by Ruth Thomas (Hutchinson,1988) brings together two unlikely misfits when they jointly discover a vast hoard of money. Adventures and problems inevitably follow; but so does self-discovery and a satisfying conclusion. Racial prejudice and intoler-ance are the theme of Mildred Taylor's *The Friendship and Other Stories* (Puffin, 1991). In Gene Kemp's *Just Ferret* (Puffin, 1991) the problem is bullying, and this time it is a dyslexic boy, Owen, who has to face up to and cope with it.

There are numerous relevant stories suitable for this age-range that take place in other lands. James Berry's *The Future-telling Lady Hamish-Hamilton, 1992) contains seven stories set in Jamaica, the title story being about Mother Esha, a healer who helps children and their parents understand and solve their problems. The Family at Ditlabeng* by Naomi Mitchison, (Collins, 1969) tells of the life of a family in rural Botswana; *The Bonus of Redunda* by Robert D Abrahams (Routledge & Kegan Paul, 1967) is an adventure story about an orphaned West Indian boy living with his grandfather in a fishing village on Nevis; V.S. Reid's *Sixty-Five* (Longmans, 1968) tells, through the eyes of a young Jamaican boy, the story of the Morant Bay rebellion of 1865 when former slaves rebelled against the plantation owners; and Andrew Salkey's *Hurricane* (OUP, 1964) is narrated from the perspective of a thirteen-year-old Jamaican boy. Still on the theme of slavery, *Marassa and Midnight* (Morna Stuart, Heinemann, 1969) deals with the revolution on the French Caribbean island of Haiti and the adventures of the twins named in the title, one of whom is taken to France while the other runs away from the plantations and lives wild in the jungle; *The Young Warriors* ((V.S.Reid, Longmans) is a fine adventure story set in Jamaica amongst the Maroons — slaves who had escaped from their white captors and who managed to form an independent community in the mountains — and featuring a group of boys coping with redcoats and other dangers to prove themselves warriors; and Martin Ballard's *Benjie's Portion* tells of a boy who joined a group of freed American slaves destined for the new British Colony of Sierra Leone.

Moving to India and the theme of 'development', Anita Desai's *The Village by the Sea* (1982) tells of the courage and perseverance of a boy and his three sisters living in a fishing village not far from Bombay, promised with (or threatened by) a major development project. Despite their mother's illness and their father's inaction the young people eventually pull through and adapt to the changes in their environment and life-style. The feast of Divali provides an important pivotal moment in Anita Desai's book; it is also the setting for *Ramu: a story of India* (Rama Mehta, Angus and Robertson, 1968) which tells of the adventures of a boy living in the ancient walled city of Udaipur. Feast-days and books provide the backbone of a nation's culture, and one of the corner-stones of Indian literary culture is the *Mahabharata*. A great modern Indian, C. Rajagopallachari, said of this work that it can be classed with the highest literature which 'transcends regionalism' and through which 'when we are properly attuned, we realise the essential oneness of the human family'. As it is a very substantial book, it is useful to have available *The Story of the Pandavas* in which Barbara Leonie (Picard Dobson, 1968) recounts the main theme of this epic for younger readers.

There are now numerous compilations of short stories written in English by writers from different cultures. The following provide a brief sample. *The Sun's Eye* (Anne Walmsley, Longmans) which also includes extracts from longer writings and poems suitable for younger secondary school pupils. This anthology contains work by some of the best known Caribbean writers. *West Indian Stories* edited by Andrew Salkey (Faber, 1960), covers a wider span so will entail more careful selection for the younger readers and listeners. *More Modern African Stories* is a collection edited by Charles R. Larson (Fontana,1975) including stories from South Africa, Ethiopia, Kenya, Senegal, Liberia and Nigeria. Black life in America is featured in the volume *Black: short story anthology* edited by Woodie King (Signet,1972). It is chiefly concerned with the revolution in Black consciousness of the 1960s and therefore centres on social protest and a renewed sense of pride and solidarity. Going back in time, six short stories by Julius Lester in *Long Journey Home* give something of the courage and poignancy of life among ordinary black people in the years leading to the Civil War in America. Ranjana Ash has produced a valuable collection, useful in secondary schools, of *Short Stories from India, Pakistan and Bangladesh* (Harrap, 1980). And a number of thought-provoking short stories by writers in various parts of the Commonwealth are gathered in an excellent anthology *Charmed Lives* selected by T.S. Dorsch (OUP 1988).

Various countries of the African continent (as elsewhere) are still experiencing revolutionary upheaval and guerrilla warfare. A long short story (or short novel) describing what it is like for a young person to be caught up in the struggle against colonialism or its after-math is published by Young World Books under the title *Nunga's Adventures* (Pepetela, 1980). There is both toughness and tenderness in this story set in the struggle for independence eventually achieved by Angola in 1975. Ngunga, its thirteen-year-old hero, has some hard decisions to make as a novice guerrilla who finally opts, for practical and unsentimental reasons, to go to school and get himself educated.

Nearer home, Joan Lingard's *Across the Barricades* (Penguin, 1975) also involves some tough decisions — this time for a Protestant girl and a Catholic boy who are determined to bridge the divide posed by sectarian hostility in Belfast. It is the story of caring people who are 'sick of bombs and people getting killed...It's not living anyway' and who 'don't want any part of it'. Their saga is continued in a number of stories culminating in *Hostages to Fortune* (Penguin, 1981).

Two challenging books by Chris Searle, *The Forsaken Lover* (Penguin, 1972) and *The World in the Classroom* (Writers and Readers Publishing Co-operative, 1977), include a good deal of prose and poetry by London secondary schoolchildren who are clearly concerned not only about their own marginalized lives but about the plight of deprived people elsewhere in the world. The class consciousness in the books is a bit heavy-handed and perhaps oversimplified, but the material provides a valuable and stimulating critique of our society with its inbuilt racism and insensitivity.

Much racism is the result of, or is exacerbated by, psychological 'projection' in which individuals or communities project their own 'shadow' (their unconscious complexes and self-rejection) upon others who provide convenient scapegoats. A fascinating fictional exploration of this phenomenon is embodied in Ursula Le Guin's *A Wizard of Earthsea* (Penguin, 1971) a fabulous tale of wizards, dragons and terrifying shadows set in a world of magic and adventure. Its hero, a boy called Sparrowhawk, acquires magical powers but is driven by pride to abuse his dangerous though potentially valuable skills. After many adventures he discovers that the enemy he has been pursuing is in fact a projection of 'the enemy within', the destructive element of his own psyche. This message is not spelt out heavy-handedly, but is subtly conveyed through the compelling action of the story. The insights provided by Le Guin's book can be a valuable antidote to the brainwashing and prejudicial attitudes to which we are all too easily subject.

Among the many travel books that can help to open the minds of young people are the adventures described by the Norwegian explorer Thor Heyerdahl in his three books: *The Kon-Tiki Expedition* (Allen and Unwin), *The Ra Expeditions* (Allen & Unwin, 1972) and *The Tigris Expedition* (Allen and Unwin 1980). Not only do these books celebrate the courage and achievements of non-European civilisations in past times, but they show how crews of different nationalities and cultures can co-operate positively in difficult and dangerous enterprises, and they reveal unexpected connections between different parts of the world in such a way as to challenge the tendency of societies and nations to divide and isolate from one another the diverse elements of our human family. The stupidity and destructiveness of war is shown up by contrast to the unity and achievement of the teams who manage their uncommon yet seaworthy craft designed on ancient models. Thor Heyerdahl's concern for humankind and the environment is clear in the conclusion to *The Ra Expedition:*

> ...it was only thanks to a common effort that we had come safely across the sea...

> We threw a last look back at the vanquished ocean.... How long would whale and fish gambol out there? Would man at the eleventh hour learn to dispose of his modern garbage, would he abandon his war against nature? Would future generations restore early man's respect and veneration for the sea and the earth, humbly worshipped by the Inca as... 'Mother Sea' and 'Mother Earth'? If not, it will be of little use to struggle for peace among nations, and still less to wage war, on board our little space-craft.

Of the world *under* the sea, writings in translation of the Frenchman, Jacques Cousteau, can provide further support regarding education for care of the environment. Before leaving this theme it is worth mentioning the little-known Manifesto of the Amerindian Chief Seattle dating from the year 1855 when the 'White Man's' Government was negotiating the acquisition of his people's land, a concept which was entirely foreign to him:

> We shall consider your offer to buy our land.
> What is it that the White Man wants to buy, my people will ask.
> It is difficult for us to understand.

> How can one buy or sell the air, the warmth of the land?
> ...If we don't own the sweet air and the bubbling water, how can you buy it from us?

> ...We are part of the earth and the earth is a part of us...

The entire Manifesto, which is both powerfully argued and yet movingly poetic, is available under the title *How Can One Sell the Air* (Book Publishing Company, Summertown, 1980, ISBN 0-913990-61-2)

d. More advanced readers

Further up in the secondary school and of course in the sixth form texts of an increasingly challenging nature can be made available. Many of the choices in the upper forms will inevitably be governed by the syllabuses for GCSE and 'A' level examinations; but even these can be progressively modified to take account of changing society, and outside of them there will remain a good deal of scope for introducing other texts either as part of courses at earlier stages, or more informally for sampling and recommending for private reading. The importance of European, Commonwealth and other literature from overseas is becoming increasingly evident. Not only is the widening of our horizons valuable from the point of view of personal culture, but from a pragmatic point of view trading and technological exchange benefit from good communications and empathy which in turn depend upon a degree of intercultural understanding. The following suggestions are largely in the nature of a catalogue of writers recommended for extending our world view and inter-national understanding generally. Examples of these should at least be in the secondary school library, and preferably find their way into the classroom at one time or another.

Africa

Elizabeth Gunnar has produced a *Handbook for Teaching African Literature* (Heinemann, 1984) to help teachers cope with difficulties of interpreting culture-bound idioms, etc. Chinua Achebe's *Things Fall Apart* (Heinemann, 1967) is probably the key text for understanding changes in African society. His *Man of the People* and *No Longer at Ease* are also recommended. Other notable Nigerian writers include Obi B Egbuna, Elechi Amadi, Chukwuemeka Ike, Amos Tutola, Cyprian Ekwensi, Festus Iyayi, J.P. Clark (Poet), Wole Soyinka (also a playwright, critic and poet) and Christopher Okigbo (poet). Ben Okri, a Nigerian writer resident in London, won the 1991 Booker Prize with his novel *The Famished Road*. Ghanaian novelists include Francis Selormey (e.g. *The Narrow Path*), Ayi Kwei Armah, Kojo Laing and Kof Anyidoho (poet). Among the many novelists from South Africa Athol Fugard, Bessie Head, Alex La Guma and Njabulo Ndebele are notable; as well as the white South African writers Alan Paton (*Cry, the Beloved Country*), Nadine Gardimer, Andre Brink and J.M. Coetzee. Other noteworthy African writers include Okot p'Bikek (Uganda), Ngugi wa Thiong'o (Kenya), Jack Mapanje (Malawi), Nuruddin Farah (Somalia), Camara Laye (French Guinea), and the white Zimbabwean writer, Doris Lessing (*The Grass is Singing*). Two anthologies of African poetry worth mentioning are *Modern Poetry from Africa* (Penguin Afri-can Library,1968), edited by Gerald Moore and Ulli Beier and *A Book of African Verse* edited by John Reed and Clive Wake (Heinemann, 1964).

India

Leaving aside the ancient classics such as the *Mahabharata* and the *Bhagavad Gita*, modern Indian writers whose works are available in English include Rabindranath Tagore, Raja Rao, Mulk Raj Anand (e.g.

Untouchable) and R.K. Narayan (e.g. *The Guide,* 1958) and the various novels set in the fictional town of Malgudi). Novelists appearing more recently on the scene include Anita Desai, Kamala Markandaya, Aran Joshi and the Polish-German-born Ruth Prawer Jhabvala. Among notable Indian poets Nissan Ezekiel, Aran Kolatkar, Adil Jussawalla and Jayanta Mahapatra write in English. Indian literature written in Bengali, Urdu, Marathi, Kannada, Tamil, Hindi, Gujarati, etc, can sometimes be found in translation, for example in the Penguin *New Writing in India* (1974), a collection of short stories, poems, etc, compiled by Adil Jussawalla. Outside of India, the Trinidadian writer, V.S. Naipaul has written a number of works on Indian themes; and Salman Rushdie, resident in England, has achieved fame with *Midnight's Children* (Pan Books, 1982) and notoriety with *The Satanic Verses* (Viking Books, 1988). For obvious reasons the latter is probably best avoided in schools for the time being; but the former, which won the Booker Prize in 1981, is generally recognised to be a *tour de force* as an imaginative critique of India's evolution since Independence.

The West Indies

For help with using literature from this area David Dabydeen's *Handbook for Teaching Caribbean Literature* (Penguin, 1992) is now available. The problems of growing up in the Caribbean are well chronicled by George Lamming (*In The Castle of My Skin*) and Samuel Selvon (in *A Brighter Sun*) from Barbados and Trinidad respectively. Also from Trinidad, V.S. Naipaul's *A House for Mr Biswas* is now a recognised classic of the West Indian scene. Other fiction writers recommended include Michael Anthony (also good on adolescents), Edward Kaman Brathwaite, Wilson Harris, R.K. Narayan, Jean Rhys, V.S. Naipaul, Shiva Naipaul, Roy Heath and Derek Walcott (who won the Nobel Prize for Literature in 1992). Notable poets, several of them resident in England, include James Berry, Linton Kwesi Johnson, Mervyn Morris and Dennis Scott (from Jamaica); Grace Nichols and David Dabydeen (from Guyana); and Claire Harris and Wayne Brown (from Trinidad). There is a useful *Penguin Book of Caribbean Verse in English* edited by Paula Burnett (1986). Much of the best Caribbean poetry, such as that by Paul Keens Douglas, Bob Morley and Linton Kwesi Johnson, is rooted in an oral tradition and is intended for reading aloud. A sampling of Kwesi Johnson's work can be found in *Dread Beat and Blood* (Bogle-L'Ouverture Publications,1975). There are inevitably various elements of Creolized English and *patois* in Caribbean poetry and prose which are both a source of interest and a challenge to the non-West Indian reader, and help is available where needed in

Dabydeen's *Handbook* mentioned above. For historical and political writing, the Trinidadian C.L.R. James is renowned and his work can be sampled, for example, in *The Future in the Present* (Alison & Busby, 1980)

This is not the place to attempt a survey of world literature. I have tried above to indicate material which is of particular concern to the make-up of our multicultural society. But we also have many people of Chinese and Japanese origin, from South America, Australia and from countries of Eastern and Western Europe living in the British Isles. It would seem to me reasonable and helpful to encourage such residents to make suggestions as to literature from their particular part of the world that is available in English, and wherever possible to make appropriate additions to our school libraries. Imaginative literature helps us to 'get inside the skin', to empathise, with people whose origins and experience are different from our own; and thus enables us to communicate and co-operate better with them to our mutual advantage.

Among helpful sources of continuing information are the monthly UNESCO *Courier*, now beautifully produced and reflecting ideas and opinions from every continent; *Bookbird*, the quarterly publication of IBBY (the International Bureau of Books for Young People) which aims to propagate news of the best books for young people from all over the world; and the Book Trust (45 East Hill, London SW18 2QZ, telephone: 081-870 9055) an educational charity which 'aims to promote reading and offers advice and information on all aspects of children's reading and books' and relevant periodicals. A periodical which carries an annual round-up of suitable new children's books in its summer issue is *Multicultural Teaching*. Also, for a non-Eurocentric perspective on 'Third World' literature, there are the quarterly journal *Third Text* published by Kala Press (303 Finchley Road, London NW3 4YR) and the subscription service (with helpful discounts) Readers International (at 8 Strathway Gardens, London NW3 4NY). Among many books introducing specifically black literature Suzanne Scafe's *Teaching Black Literature* (Kogan Page, 1989) will be found useful.

Chapter 10

Conclusion: What of the Future?

Very little is to be gained by sitting in judgement upon the errors of the past. It is more profitable to collect our thoughts and devise ways and means by which we shall be able to avoid future mistakes.... For better or worse this planet has become one large going concern.... We no longer live in a world the future of which can take care of itself.
(Hendrik Van Loon, The Home of Mankind, 1933)

Human history becomes more and more a race between education and catastrophe.
(H G Wells, The Outline of History, 1951)

We cannot always build the future for our youth, but we can build our youth for the future.
(Franklin D Roosevelt, 1940)

Whatever our dreams and visions may be, there is no escaping facts; and we have two stubborn facts to contend with. One, that we now have *de facto* a National Curriculum whether we like it or not; and the other, that the world for which the curriculum must seek to prepare our youth is an interdependent yet uncertain, volatile and in many places violent one. The preceding chapters have been an attempt to explore, and where possible indicate, the compatibility of these two facts.

Considering society in its widest sense — as global society — can we say that the National Curriculum fulfils the requirements of Section One of the Education Reform Act 1988 to provide 'a broad and balanced curriculum which

— 'promotes the spiritual, moral, cultural, mental and physical development of pupils at the school and of society (and)

— prepares pupils for the opportunities, responsibilities and experiences of adult life'?

In my view the answer is a qualified 'yes'. Qualified because the National Curriculum is open to a range of interpretations. This is both a strength and a weakness. A strength because guidelines are better for teachers than straitjackets, which simply stifle creativity; a weakness because a teacher with narrow horizons and materialistic, short-term, self-seeking attitudes could concentrate on those areas of the curriculum which support such an outlook and ignore the many openings for a broader, more humane and long-term view.

An Indian teacher in North London, driving her Toyota to school might well smile were she to tune in to her Sony transistor and catch a reading of the Kipling poem quoted earlier — 'Oh, East is East and West is West / And never the twain shall meet'! Kipling is long dead, and so is that world. Anyone denying it is living in a cocoon, though the mental habits belonging to that world die hard. The need to educate the coming generation for intercultural tolerance and international understanding is clear, as are the urgent needs to understand and cope with conflict, and to acquire habits of mutual co-operation in preference to crude competition.

We have an obligation under Article 26(2) of the Universal Declaration of Human Rights to ensure that the education of our youth meets certain standards, not simply from a sense of high-flown idealism, but because the real world will demand such standards if it is to be worth living in. And we must ask of every subject in the National Curriculum how far it can help to promote those standards — through the arts and science subjects, through religious education, through citizenship and through physical education. The Article in question should be displayed in every staffroom. If we could really live up to it the tragic waste of Northern Ireland could be eliminated and we could begin steadily to reduce some of the inequalities and injustices in the world at large. Certainly the objectives of the National Curriculum are not in conflict with 'the strengthening of respect for Human Rights and fundamental freedoms', with the promotion of 'understanding, tolerance and friendship among nations, racial or religious groups' and the other objectives of Article 26(2); but (considering the times we live in) they are not spelt out as forcibly as they might be, and it is up to teachers to bring out the best in the curriculum.

There is a long-standing myth about French education — that in France the national curriculum requires every child of a particular standard to be doing exactly the same thing as his or her contemporary at every hour across the country. Anyone who has spent time in a French school knows that this is not so. The curriculum is there, but it has been in place long enough to be digested. (In England, schools are still suffering from curricular indigestion, and will continue to do so for a while to come.) I well remember one particular happy afternoon spent in a French state primary school answering to the best of my ability the innumerable lively questions put to me about England by enthusiastic pupils. At the end of the afternoon I asked the teacher to show me the national curriculum he was working to. 'I think it's in the cupboard somewhere,' he said. But although he searched for it for some time he wasn't able to lay his hands on it that afternoon. Subsequent visits to French primary and secondary schools have confirmed my impression that their national curriculum is not the ogre that it might once have been and is still imagined abroad to be. Hard as it may be to believe, the same thing will almost certainly happen to our own National Curriculum in due course. At the moment it is like a carapace, an outer shell restricting and slowing down movement; but by natural evolution it will gradually become more of a skeleton, a frame providing an overall shape to the work in our schools but agreeably fleshed out and facilitating movement and exploration.

On the whole, therefore, I think the institution of a national curriculum is a worthwhile development: it is better than indifference or anarchy. My objections are largely to the way in which it has been introduced — too much, too quickly and too clumsily. In the foregoing pages I have on several occasions criticised our Secretaries of State for

Education. The succession of ministers who have come and gone during the installation of the National Curriculum have, with few exceptions, shown an insensitivity to the teachers who throughout it all have borne the heat and burden of the day in the classrooms. It is all very well for highly-paid public servants holding office for a few months, or a year or so at most, to make *ex cathedra* pronouncements over the heads of the specialists and practitioners whose experience gained over years they ignore. No wonder morale among teachers has been at a low ebb this past decade! In favour of some of the actions of Secretaries of State it must be admitted that they have wisely simplified some over-complex programmes. But against this, it has to be said that too much had been asked of the National Curriculum Council's subject committees in the first place. Furthermore, when simplifying reductions have been made, these have often been at the expense of the more farseeing and liberal elements in the programmes in question.

Be that as it may, we now have a curriculum and when the nonsense of league-table testing has been finally swept away — as in due course it must be — teachers will have a good base to work from. On the subject of testing, everybody knows that testing of one kind or another has an important role to play in education — particularly diagnostic testing and the testing of knowledge and skills to undertake further studies or to enter certain fields of employment. But the league-table testing of schools, via pupils' results, is a meaningless exercise that could serve no educational purpose. It would be about as much use as the productivity charts on the factory floors of former communist countries: figures bearing no relation to the entities they purport to represent. Or worse, one can imagine a market-oriented education system where heads and governors of schools, like league football club committees, buy and sell teachers with reputations for getting high marks for their pupils' tests! This is one aspect of the National Curriculum that could have served neither international nor national education. It is a nonstarter and belongs to a competitive, mechanistic ideology that is now fortunately more and more open to question.

Some interesting research into social values is reported by Francis Kinsman in *Millennium: Towards Tomorrow's Society* (1990) which suggests that there is a growing number of people who are 'less materialistic' and 'more concerned with ethics' than with maintaining their status quo or seeking 'power or influence'. They reject the exploitative values of the past, are more ecologically aware, and recognise that sustainable growth — based on economic relationships

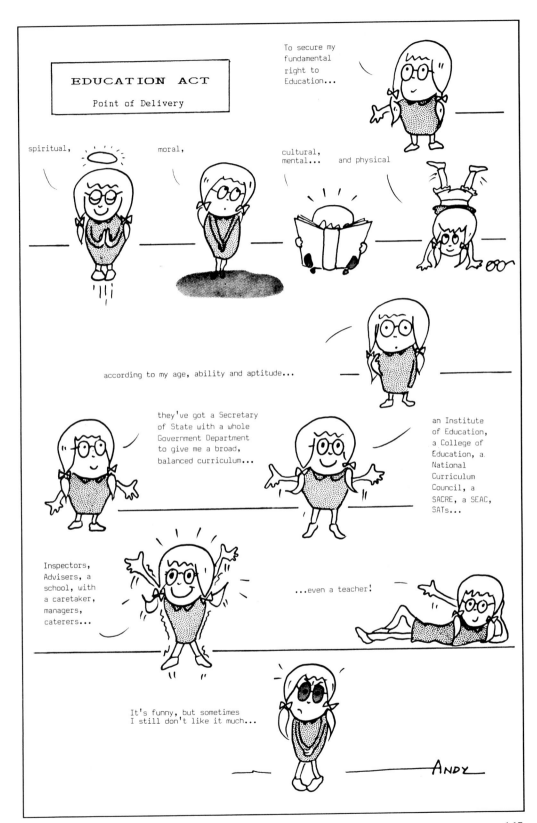

that can last into the future — depends upon a holistic outlook. This tendency is encouraging, and if it proves to be continuing, augurs well for the future.

Kinsman's research is discussed in David Hicks's *Exploring Alternative Futures* (1991) where he suggests that:

> We may...be due for an extended period of uncertainty, conflict and turbulence as these two stories compete for our attention and allegiance, the old mechanistic worldview with its emphasis on progress at all costs v. the newer holistic worldview with its emphasis on sustainability. How long (he asks) does it take historically for one story to replace another?

A difficult question to answer; but perhaps education can help speed up the process. In the same book David Hicks discusses the importance of images of the future if we are to have clear ideas as to our direction:

> ...we can most easily work towards the future we prefer (he suggests) if we have clear images of where we want to go and how we might get there. If we can share the process of envisioning these futures with others we also enhance their creative power, whether at individual, local or societal levels.

I hope that the present book, as well as offering a number of criticism of the past, has offered some positive images and ideas for teachers concerned to work towards a more hopeful and peaceful future. I hope I have shown, too, that there are plenty of openings for this within the framework of the National Curriculum. For the sake of our children and of future generations, it is up to us to make the best use we can of these openings.

Appendix 1

Universal Declaration of Human Rights

On December 10, 1948, the General Assembly of the United Nations adopted and proclaimed the Universal Declaration of Human Rights, the full text of which appears below. Following this historic act the Assembly called upon all Member countries to publicise the text of the Declaration and 'to cause it to be disseminated, displayed, read and expounded principally in schools and other educational institutions....'

Universal Declaration of Human Rights
Preamble

Whereas recognition of the inherent dignity and of the equal and inalienable rights of all members of the human family is the foundation of freedom, justice and peace in the world,

Whereas disregard and contempt for human rights have resulted in barbarous acts which have outraged the conscience of mankind, and the advent of a world in which human beings shall enjoy freedom of speech and belief and freedom from fear and want has been proclaimed as the highest aspiration of the common people,

Whereas it is essential, if man is not to be compelled to have recourse, as a last resort, to rebellion against tyranny and oppression, that human rights should be protected by the rule of law,

Whereas it is essential to promote the development of friendly relations between nations,

Whereas the peoples of the United Nations have in the Charter reaffirmed their faith in fundamental human rights, in the dignity and worth of the human person and in the equal rights of men and women and have determined to promote social progress and better standards of life in larger freedom,

Whereas Member States have pledged themselves to achieve, in co-operation with the United Nations, the promotion of universal respect for and observance of human rights and fundamental freedoms,

Whereas a common understanding of these rights and freedoms is of the greatest importance for the full realisation of this pledge,

Now, therefore,

THE GENERAL ASSEMBLY

proclaims

THIS UNIVERSAL DECLARATION OF HUMAN RIGHTS as a common standard of achievement for all peoples and all nations, to the end that every individual and every organ of society, keeping this Declaration constantly in mind, shall strive by teaching and education to promote respect for these rights and freedoms and by progressive measures, national and international, to secure their universal and effective recognition and observance, both among the peoples of Member States themselves and among the peoples of territories under their jurisdiction.

Article 1. All human beings are born free and equal in dignity and rights. They are endowed with reason and conscience and should act towards one another in a spirit of brotherhood.

Article 2. Everyone is entitled to all the rights and freedoms set forth in this Declaration, without distinction of any kind, such as race, colour, sex, language, religion, political or other opinion, national or social origin, property, birth or other status.

Furthermore, no distinction shall be made on the basis of the political, jurisdictional or international status of the country or territory to which a person belongs, whether it be independent, trust, non-self-governing or under any other limitation of sovereignty.

Article 3. Everyone has the right to life, liberty and the security of the person.

Article 4. No one shall be held in slavery or servitude; slavery and the slave trade shall be prohibited in all their forms.

Article 5. No one shall be subjected to torture or to cruel, inhuman or degrading treatment or punishment.

Article 6. Everyone has the right to recognition everywhere as a person before the law.

Article 7. All are equal before the law and are entitled without any discrimination to equal protection of the law. All are entitled to equal protection against any discrimination in violation of this Declaration and against any incitement to such discrimination.

Article 8. Everyone has the right to an effective remedy by the competent national tribunals for acts violating the fundamental rights granted him by the constitution or by law.

Article 9. No one shall be subjected to arbitrary arrest, detention or exile.

Article 10. Everyone is entitled in full equality to a fair and public hearing by an independent and impartial tribunal, in the determination of his rights and obligations and of any criminal charge against him.

Article 11. (1) Everyone charged with a penal offence has the right to be presumed innocent until proved guilty according to law in a public trial at which he has had all the guarantees necessary for his defence.

(2) No one shall be held guilty of any penal offence on any account of any act or omission which did not constitute a penal offence, under national or international law, at the time when it was committed. Nor shall a heavier penalty be imposed than the one that was applicable at the time the penal offence was committed.

Article 12. No one shall be subjected to arbitrary interference with his privacy, family, home or correspondence, nor to attacks upon his honour and reputation. Everyone has the right to the protection of the law against such interference or attacks.

Article 13. (1) Everyone has the right to freedom of movement and residence within the borders of each state.

(2) Everyone has the right to leave any country, including his own, and to return to his country.

Article 14. (1) Everyone has the right to seek and enjoy in other countries asylum from persecution.

(2) This right may not be invoked in the case of prosecutions genuinely arising from non-political crimes or from acts contrary to the purposes and principles of the United Nations.

Article 15. (1) Everyone has the right to a nationality.

(2) No one shall be arbitrarily deprived of his nationality nor denied the right to change his nationality.

Article 16. (1) Men and women of a full age, without any limitation due to race, nationality or religion, have the right to marry and to found a family. They are entitled to equal rights as to marriage, during marriage and at its dissolution.

(2) Marriage shall be entered into only with the free and full consent of the intending spouses.

(3) The family is the natural and fundamental group unit of society and is entitled to protection by society and the State.

Article 17. (1) Everyone has the right to own property alone as well as in association with others.

(2) No one shall be arbitrarily deprived of his property.

Article 18. Everyone has the right to freedom of thought, conscience and religion; this right includes the freedom to change his religion or belief, and freedom, either alone or in community with others and in public or private, to manifest his religion or belief in teaching, practice, worship and observance.

Article 19. Everyone has the right to freedom of opinion and expression; this right includes freedom to hold opinions without interference and to seek, receive and impart information and ideas through any media regardless of frontiers.

Article 20. (1) Everyone has the right to freedom of peaceful assembly and association.

(2) No one may be compelled to belong to an association.

Article 21. (1) Everyone has the right to take part in the government of his country, directly or through freely chosen representatives.

(2) Everyone has the right of equal access to public service in his country.

(3) The will of the people shall be the basis of the authority of government; this will shall be expressed in periodic and genuine elections which shall be by universal suffrage and shall be held by secret vote or by equivalent free voting procedures.

Article 22. Everyone, as a member of society, has the right to social security and is entitled to realisation, through national effort and international co-operation and in accordance with the organisation and resources of each

State, of the economic, social and cultural rights indispensable for his dignity and the free development of his personality.

Article 23. (1) Everyone has the right to work, to free choice of employment, to just and favourable conditions of work and to protection against unemployment.

(2) Everyone, without any discrimination, has the right to equal pay for equal work.

(3) Everyone who works has the right to just and favourable remuneration ensuring for himself and his family an existence worthy of human dignity, and supplemented, if necessary, by other means of social protection.

(4) Everyone has the right to join trade unions for the protection of his interests.

Article 24. Everyone has the right to rest and leisure, including reasonable limitation of working hours and periodic holidays with pay.

Article 25. (1) Everyone has the right to a standard of living adequate for the health and well-being of himself and his family, including food, clothing, housing and medical care and necessary social services, and the right to security in the event of unemployment, sickness, disability, widowhood, old age or other lack of livelihood in circumstances beyond his control.

(2) Motherhood and childhood are entitled to special care and assistance. All children, whether born in or out of wedlock, shall enjoy the same social protection.

Article 26. (1) Everyone has the right to education. Education shall be free, at least in the elementary and fundamental stages. Elementary education shall be compulsory. Technical and professional education shall be made generally available and higher education shall be equally accessible to all on the basis of merit.

(2) Education shall be directed to the full development of the human personality and to the strengthening of respect for human rights and fundamental freedoms. It shall promote understanding, tolerance and friendship among all nations, racial or religious groups, and shall further the activities of the United Nations for the maintenance of peace.

(3) Parents have a prior right to choose the kind of education that shall be given to their children.

Article 27. 9(1) Everyone has the right freely to participate in the cultural life of the community, to enjoy the arts and to share in scientific advancement and its benefits.

(2) Everyone has the right to the protection of the moral and material interests resulting from any scientific, literary or artistic production of which he is the author.

Article 28. Everyone is entitled to a social and international order in which the rights and freedoms set forth in this Declaration can be fully realised.

Article 29. (1) Everyone has duties to the community in which alone the free and full development of his personality is possible.

(2) In the exercise of his rights and freedoms, everyone shall be subject only to such limitations as are determined by law solely for the purpose of securing due recognition and respect for the rights and freedoms of others and of meeting the just requirements of morality, public order, and the general welfare in a democratic society.

(3) These rights and freedoms may in no case be exercised contrary to the purposes and principles of the United Nations.

Article 30. Nothing in this Declaration may be interpreted as implying for any State, group or person any right to engage in any activity or to perform any act aimed at the destruction of any of the rights and freedoms set forth herein.

Appendix 2

The Seville Statement on Violence

(a Unesco abridgement written in plain words)

The Statement was written in Seville, Spain, in 1986, for the International Year of Peace. Scientists met to answer the question: 'Do modern biology and the social sciences know of any biological factors that are insurmountable or serious obstacles to the goal of world peace?' The scientists assembled brought together for consideration many studies about animal behaviour, psychology, brain research, genetics and other related issues. Their conclusions (summarised below) have been endorsed by many organisations of scientists, among others the International Society for Research on Aggression, the International Council of Psychologists, the American Anthropological, Psychological, and Sociological Associations, and the Psychological Societies of Denmark and New Zealand.

It was felt that such a Statement was needed because a number of scientific studies have shown that some 50% of young people believe in the myth that war and violence are inherent in human nature, and these young people are consequently less likely to take part in action for peace.

Introduction

The Statement is a message of hope. It says that peace is possible and that wars and violence can be ended. It was written by scientists from many countries, North, South, East and West, and has been endorsed and published by many organisations of scientists around the world.

The problem of war and violence has been studied with today's scientific methods. Although conclusions in science are never final, scientists have a responsibility to speak out on the basis of the latest information.

Some people say that war and violence cannot be ended because they are part of our biology. That is not true. People used to justify slavery as well as racial and sexist domination by claiming that they are biological and inevitable. But they were wrong. Slavery has been ended and now the world is working to end racial and sexist domination.

Five Propositions

1. It is scientifically incorrect to say that war cannot be ended because animals make war and because people are like animals. First, it is not true because animals do not make war. Second, it is not true because unlike animals people have culture and the ability to change their culture. A culture that makes war in one century may change and live in peace with its neighbours in another century.

2. It is scientifically incorrect to say that war cannot be ended because it is part of human nature. Arguments about human nature cannot prove anything because human culture gives people the ability to shape and change their nature from one generation to another.

3. It is scientifically incorrect to say that violence cannot be ended because people and animals who are violent are able to live better and reproduce more than others. Actually, the evidence shows that people and animals do best when they learn to work well with each other.

4. It is scientifically incorrect to say that people must be violent because of their brain. The brain is like other parts of the body. They can all be used for co-operation as well as for violence. All depends on the purpose of their use.

5. It is scientifically incorrect to say that war is caused by 'instinct'. Most scientists do not use the word 'instinct' any more because behaviour is not determined to the point that it cannot be changed by learning. Of course, everyone has emotions but, in modern war, decisions and actions are not necessarily emotional.

Conclusion

Biology does not condemn humanity to violence and war. Instead, it is possible to end war and the suffering it causes. To do this will require everyone working together, but it must begin in the mind of each person with the belief that it is possible. The same human being who has made war is capable of constructing peace. Each of us has a task to do.

(The original Seville Statement, along with a scientific bibliography and a complete list of endorsing organisations, is published in the UNESCO brochure, The Seville Statement on Violence.*)*

Bibliography

Chapter One

Commonwealth Institute (1991). Commonwealth Heads of Government Meeting Harare: News release. Commonwealth Institute 19-22 October 1991.

DES (1987). The National Curriculum 5-16: a consultation document. DES.

DES (1989). National Curriculum: from Policy to Practice. DES.

DES (1991). Testing 7 year olds in 1991: the results of the National Curriculum assessments in England. DES.

Hargreaves, J A (1970). Computers, Education and a World of Change. University of London Institute of Education Bulletin, No.21, Summer 1979.

Lane, Jane (1992). 'The 1989 Children Act: a framework for racial equality in children's day care' in Multicultural Teaching vol.10, no.1, September 1992.

NCC (1990). Education for Citizenship (Curriculum Guidance, No. 8). NCC.

Snow, C P (1964). The Two Cultures. Mentor Books.

UN (1948). Universal Declaration of Human Rights. (see Appendix)

UNESCO (1974). Recommendation concerning Education for International Understanding, Co-operation and Peace and Education relating to Human Rights and Fundamental Freedoms adopted by the General Conference at its 18th session. Unesco Paris.

Wall, W D (1977). Constructive Education for Adolescents. Harrap/Unesco.

Chapter Two

DES (1990). National Curriculum History Working Group Final Report. DES, April, 1990.

DES (1991). History in the National Curriculum. HMSO, March 1991

Fromm, Eric (1942). The Fear of Freedom. Routledge & Kegan Paul.

Gorbachev, Mikhail (1988). Address at the United Nations. Moscow: Novosti Press Agency Publishing House.

Gorbachev, Mikhail (1987). Perestroika. New Thinking for our Country and the World. New York, Harper and Row.

Hicks, David (1991). Exploring Alternative Futures. Global Futures Project, Institute of Education, University of London.

Poppleton, P et al (1990). 'Perestroika and the Soviet Teachers' in New Era in Education, vol.71, no.3, December 1990.

Chapter Three

DES (1990). English in the National Curriculum (No. 2). HMSO.

DES (1988). Report of the Committee of Inquiry into the Teaching of the English Language (under the Chairmanship of Sir John Kingman). HMSO.

DFE (1993). English for ages 5 to 16 (1993): Proposals of the Secretary of State for Education and the Secretary of State for Wales. NCC, April 1993.

Hayakawa, S I (1966). Language in Thought and Action. Allen & Unwin.

Masheder, Mildred (1986). Let's Co-operate. PPU Peace Education Project, London.

Potter, Simeon (1961). Language in the Modern World. Penguin Books.

Prutzman, Priscilla et al (1978). The Friendly Classroom for a Small Planet. USA, Avery Publishing Group Inc.

Stubbs, Michael (1990). Knowledge About Language. Institute of Education, University of London.

Whitehead, Frank (1966). The Disappearing Dais. Chatto and Windus.

Chapter Four

Adams, Russell L (1969) Great Negroes Past and Present. Afro-American Publishing Co. Inc. Chicago.

Bronowski, Jacob (1976). The Ascent of Man. BBC.

CWDE (Council for World Development Education) at 1 Catton Street, London WC1R 4AB, issues various relevant catalogues, fact-sheets, software, etc.

DES (1988). Mathematics for Ages 5-16: Proposals of the Secretary of State for Education. HMSO.

DES (1989). Mathematics in the National Curriculum. HMSO.

DES (1987). The National Curriculum 5-16: a consultation document. DES, July 1987.

DES (1988). National Curriculum: Science for ages 5-16 (Science Working Group). DES

DES (1989). Science in the National Curriculum. HMSO

Hogben, Lancelot (1989). Mathematics for the Million. The Marlin Press.

Hollingdale, Stuart (1989). Makers of Mathematics. Penguin Books.

McLeish, John (1992). Number: from Ancient Civilizations to the Computer. Flamingo (Harper/Collins).

Mead, Margaret (1972). Culture and Commitment. Panther Books

Shah, Sharon-Jeet & Bailey, Peter (1991). Multiple Factors: Classroom Mathematics for Equality and Justice. Trentham Books.

Unesco (November, 1989). 'A Mathematical Mystery Tour' in The Courier. Unesco.
Unesco (April, 1991). 'Perceptions of Time' in The Courier. Unesco.

Chapter Five

A.

Brandt, Willy et al (1980). North-South: a programme for survival. Pan Books

Hicks, David (1981). Bias in Geography Textbooks. Centre for Multicultural Education, Institute of Education, University of London.

Hicks, David (1980). Images of the World: an introduction to bias in teaching materials. Centre for Multicultural Education, Institute of Education, University of London.

James, C L R (1980). The Future in the Present. Allison & Busby.

Kent, Ashley & Slater, Francis (1989). An International Dimension in the National Curriculum: an imperative for Britain for 1992 and beyond (A Report of a Conference held at the Institute of Education, University of London on 23-24th January 1989).

Klein, Gillian (1985). Reading into Racism. Routledge & Kegan Paul.

Preiswerk, Roy (Ed) (1981). The Slant of the Pen: racism in children's books. World Council of Churches, Geneva.

B.

De Bono, Edward (1972). Children Solve Problems. Allen Lane Penguin Press.

DES (1989). Technology in the National Curriculum. HMSO.

DFE (1992). Technology for ages 5-16: proposals of the Secretary of State for Education.. National Curriculum Council.

McRobie, George (1981). Small is Possible. Abacus/Sphere Books.

Schumacher, E F (1974). Small is Beautiful. Abacus/Sphere Books.

C.

Aplin, Richard et al (1985). Orientations. Hodder & Stoughton.

Cohen, Jacqueline & Despres, Bernadette (1985). Tom-Tom et ses Idees Explosive. Bayard Press, Paris.

DES (1991). Modern Foreign Languages. HMSO

Ducamp, Jean-Louis (1984). Les Droits de l'Homme Raconte aux Enfants. Editions Ouvrieres, Paris.

Ferguson, M et al (apres Hector Malot) (1992). Sans Famille. Editions.Bayard.

Filippini, Henri (1989). Dictionnaire de la Bande Dessinee. Bordos, Paris.

Haycroft, John (1978). An Introduction to English Language Teaching. Longmans Group.

Jean, Georges (1984). Le Racisme Raconte aux Enfants. Editions Ouvrieres, Paris.

Moreau, Jean-Luc (1986). La Liberte Raconte aux Enfants. Editions Ouvrieres, Paris.

Unicef (1989). Prete-moi Ta Plume... Castor Poche Flammarion.

Chapter Six

A.

Bernal, M (1986). 'The Afro-asaic Roots of Classical Civilization' in Black Athene, London, Freedom of Association Press.

DFE (1992). National Curriculum: Draft Order for Art. DFE.

DFE (Summer 1992). Schools Update. DFE, NCC & SEAC.

deSouza, Allan (1991). 'Sublime Differences' in Distinguishing Marks. ILEA Equal Opportunity Unit and the Centre for Multicultural Education, Institute of Education, University of London.

Gundara, Jagdish (1987). Art Education in a Multicultural Society, unpublished conference paper given in Bergen, the Netherlands. Centre for Multicultural Education, Institute of Education, University of London.

Sarup, Madan (1991). Education and the Ideologies of Racism. Trentham Books.

Semple, Maggie (1991). 'Black Artist as a Resource' in Distinguishing Marks. (v. supra.)

B.

DFE (1992). National Curriculum: Draft Order for Music. DFE.

Silverman, Jerry (1968). Folk Blues. New York, Macmillan Co.

C.

Carrington, B. (1982) 'Sport as a side-track; an analysis of West Indian involvement in extra-curriculuar sport' in Barton, L. and Walker, S. (eds): Race, Class and Education. Croom Helm.

DFE (1992). National Curriculum: Draft Order for Physical Education. DFE.

Forster, E M (1957). Two Cheers for Democracy. Penguin Books.

Unesco (November 1988). Final Report of the Intergovernmental Committee for Physical Education and Sport. Unesco, Moscow.

Unesco (November 1988). Final Report on the Second International Conference of Ministers and Senior Officials Responsible for Physical Education and Sport. Unesco, Moscow.

Chapter Seven

DES, NCC & SEAC (1989). Circular No. 3/89: The Education Reform Act: Religious Education and Collective Worship. DES.

DES (1977). Curriculum 11-16: Working Papers by HM Inspectorate: a contribution to current debate. DES.

Gundara, Jagdish (December 1989). Issues for Education and Community Relations. Unpublished paper presented at Council of Europe Conference, Strasbourg.

Kaunda, Kenneth (1973). Letter to my Children. Longmans.

Leimdorfer, Tom (1991). 'Warsaw Snapshots' in The Friend, vol.149, no.26, 28 June 1991.

NCC (1992). Analysis of SACRE Reports. NCC.

NCC (November 1990). Education for Citizenship. NCC.

Chapter Eight

Arnold, Matthew (1971). Culture and Anarchy. (1869) edited by J Dover Wilson. Cambridge University Press.

DES (1990). English in the National Curriculum (No.2). HMSO.

DFE (1993). English for ages 5 to 16 (1993). DFE April 1993.

Gundara, Jagdish (ed.) (1987). Educational opportunities for access to literature written in less well-known European languages and literature written in Africa, Asia and the Caribbean. (Unpublished documents for Unesco Contract no. 700.316.5.)

Niven, Alastair (1987). 'Literature from the English-speaking countries in Africa, Asia and the Caribbean in the United Kingdom' in Gundara (ed.) (1987) cited above.

Owen, Wilfred (1963). The Collected Poems of Wilfred Owen (edited with an introduction and notes by C Day Lewis). Chatto & Windus.

Scafe, Suzanne (1989). Teaching Black Literature. Virago Press.

Sillitoe, Alan (1962). The Loneliness of the Long-Distance Runner. Pan Books.

Solzhenitsyn, Alexander (1973). Solzhenitsyn Nobel Prize Lecture. Stenvalley Press (pp.29 & 51)

Chapter Nine

DES (1990) and DFE (1993) see references for Chapter Eight above.

Dabydeen, David (1992). Handbook for Teaching Caribbean Literature. Penguin Books.

Gunnar, Elizabeth (1984). Handbook for Teaching African Literature. Heinemann.

Klein, Gillian (1985). Reading into Racism. Routledge & Kegan Paul.

Note. References to the many works recommended in the chapter are given in the text.

Chapter Ten

Hicks, David (1991). Exploring Alternative Futures: a Teacher's Interim Guide. Global Futures Project, Institute of Education, Univesity of London.

Kinsman, F (1990). Millennium: Towards Tomorrow's Society. W H Allen.

General

Andrews, Rex (1988). 'Educating for a Future; symbols of life and hope' in Towards a Renaissance of Humanity (ed. T R Carson). World Council for Curriculum and Instruction/University of Alberta.

Andrews, Rex (1988). 'Unesco Rethinks its Future' in New Era in Education, vol. 69, no. 2, August 1988.

Andrews, Rex (1990). 'Towards the Twenty-first Century with Unesco' in New Era in Education, vol. 71, no.2, August 1990.

Council for World Development Education (1992). The CWDE Worldaware Catalogue 1992.

Cooke, Dave et al (1985). Teaching Development Issues. Section 1: Perceptions. Development Education Project, Manchester.

Cooke, Dave et al (1985). Teaching Development Issues. Section 2: Colonialism. Development Education Project, Manchester.

Cox, John (1976). On the Warpath. OUP

DES (1985). Better Schools. White Paper Cmnd 9469. HMSO

Fyson, Nance Jui (1984). The Development Puzzle. (CWDE) Hodder & Stoughton.

Heater, Derek (1985). Our World Today. OUP.

Kapo, Remi (1981). A Savage Culture: racism — a black British view. Quartet Books.

Keen, Sam (1986). Faces of the Enemy. Harper & Row, USA.

Leeds, Chris (1987). Peace and War: a first sourcebook. Stanley Thorne.

Myers, Norman (ed) (1985). The Gaia Atlas of Planet Management. Pan Books.

Pax Christi (1980). Winners All: co-operative games for all ages. Pax Christi.

Pettman, Ralph (1984). Teaching for Human Rights. Australia: Hodja Education Resources Co-operative.

Rabinowitz, Ralph (1991). What is War? What is Peace? — 50 questions and answers for kids. USA, Byron Preiss/Avon Camelot Books.

Richardson, Robin (1980). World in Conflict. Nelson.

Sengova, Theresa (1988). Teaching Guidelines for a Small World. Marc Goldstein Memorial Trust, Centre for Multicultural Education, Institute of Education, University of London.

Shillington, Kevin (1989). History of Africa. Macmillan.

Unesco (1991). Ecology Chronicle: 24 Windows on the Man and the Biosphere Programme. Unesco.

Unesco (1993). Unesco: Programmes and Priorities 1992-1993. Unesco, Paris.

Woodhouse, Sara (1980). Your Life, My Life: an introduction to Human Rights and Responsibilities. Writers and Scholars Educational Trust.

Journals

Multicultural Teaching published termly by Trentham Books.

New Era in Education. Termly journal of the World Education Fellowship.

Unesco Courier. (Monthly)

Unesco Sources. (Monthly)

Nature and Resources. Unesco quarterly.

(Note. Address of Unesco for these and other publications: Unesco, 7 Place de Fontenoy, 75700 PARIS.)

Index

African literature 157

Arms Race 12

Arnold, Matthew 6

Assemblies (see also 'Worship') 119

Athletics 102

Athletic records 105

Attainment Targets 6, 16, 43

Balance 5

Bias 36, 68

Bill of rights 125

Biography 151

Blues 98

'Broad traditions of Christian belief' 117

Callaghan, Sir James 4

Chemistry 53

Children Act 9

Christianity 111, 116

Citizenship 7, 110, 121

'Civilisation' 123

Close reading 138

Commonwealth 9, 132, 134

Commonwealth literature 130

Communication 28

Community, the idea of 122

Compromise 125

Consensus, negotiating 31

Context, historical 139

Co-operation 30

Council of Europe 8

Creativity 86, 92

Creole 131

Culture 132

Demeaning language 68

Dance 102

Democracy (in action) 122

Development 66, 70

Disagreement 31

Dogmatic teaching 129

Discrimination 35

Education Reform Act 5

English culture 128

English language 28

Environmental issues 79

Ethnicity 123

Ethnocentricity 133

Eurocentrism 68, 87, 95

European Community 132

Folk tales 147

Foreign language, acquisition of 80

Foreign language-learning texts 82

Foreign stamps 45

Functional language-learning 81

French National Curriculum 163

Fundamentalism 115

Games 103

Gandhi, M K 118, 136

Glasnost 4, 12, 16, 25

Global Citizenship 7

Grammar 35, 38

Gymnastics 102

History, interpretation of 19

History, use of sources 20

Human Rights 110, 115

Human Rights, Universal
  Declaration of 2, 9, 125, 162

Ideological teaching 129

Imaginative literature 129

Indian literature 157

Indo-European, language family
  40

Intermediate technology 73

International sport 104

Jazz 98

Justification theories of 69

Kipling, Rudyard 136

Kaunda, Dr Kenneth 119

Language-mastery 33

Language, borrowings from other
  languages 39

Language changes 39

'League-table' testing 164

Life-forms 52

Literature, principles of choice 127,
  140

Literature, range of material 143

'Mainstream' literature 131

Mathematics, historical approach
  47

Mathematics, 'pure' and 'applied'
  45

Minority-group membership 130

Mother tongue 33

Multi-faith and multi-ethnic
  communities 114

Museum visits 93

Music, listening and appraising 98

Music-making (performing and
  composing) 96, 97

Musical history 96

Myths and legends 147

'National culture', 133, 134

National Curriculum
  Art 86
  Citizenship 121
  English 28
  Geography Programme 62
  History Programme 16, 17
  Mathematics Programme 44
  Modern Foreign Language 80
  Music 94
  Physical Education 101
  Religious Education 110
  Science Programme 51
  Technology (& Design) 72

Nationalism 124

Nationhood, the sense of 122

Olympic Games 104

Openmindedness not
  empty-mindedness 125

Outdoor and adventurous
  activities 102

Participation 30

Payment by Results 6

Perestroika 12, 15, 25

Physical health 101

Physics 55

Poetry writing 41

Postage stamp designing 92

Prejudice 56

Problem-solving 76

Programmes of study 43

Race and physical skills 106

Religious Education 110

Religious Education, shortage of
  teachers 120

Religious language 111

Samizdat 12

Right to withdraw 111

Science, limitations of 55

Science, methods and processes 57

Secretaries of State for Education 163

Secular education, arguments for 112

Self-image (and self-knowledge) 123, 130

Seville Statement on Violence 53

Short stories 154

Speaking and listening 28

Specialisation 4

Standard English 33, 35

Sustainable development 73

Swimming 102

Syncretism 88

Tests, national 6

'Third World' 68, 70

'Third World' literature 139

Tolerance 115, 124

Tolerance of uncertainty and diversity 130

Tolstoy, Leo 117

Travel books 155

Two-valued orientation 30

Unesco 4, 49, 68, 71, 101, 104, 119, 159

Unesco General Conference 8

United Nations 14

Values education and Value 121, 129 systems

Violence 53

War, attitudes to 3

War, language of 103

Warsaw Pact, former countries of 14

West Indian literature 158

'Western Classical Tradition' 87

World faiths 110

Worship, daily (collective) act of 111, 117

Writing, stories and other subject-matter 40

Writing, acquisition of 33